Brief Lives:
Joseph Conrad

Brief Lives:
Joseph Conrad

Gavin Griffiths

ET REMOTISSIMA PROPE

Brief Lives
Published by Hesperus Press Limited
4 Rickett Street, London sw6 1ru
www.hesperuspress.com

First published by Hesperus Press Limited, 2008

Designed and typeset by Fraser Muggeridge studio
Printed in Jordan by Jordan National Press

isbn: 978-1-84391-907-0

Contents

Poland
1856–74

And I see a bay, a wide bay, smooth as glass and polished like ice, shimmering in the dark. A red light burns far off upon the gloom of the land, and the night is soft and warm. We drag at the oars with aching arms, and suddenly a puff of wind, a puff faint and tepid and laden with strange odours of blossoms, of aromatic wood, comes out of the still night – the first sigh of the East on my face. That I can never forget. It was impalpable and enslaving, like a charm, like a whispered promise of mysterious delight.

'Youth'

Conrad's short story 'Youth' was semi-autobiographical. When Richard Curle, friend and critic, rooted around to uncover the facts behind the fiction, Conrad was apoplectic. Curle was pleased to have discovered that Conrad's final destination was Muntok.

Conrad replied:

The paragraph you quote of the East meeting the narrator is all right in itself; whereas directly it's connected with Muntok it becomes nothing at all. Muntok is a damned hole without any beach and without any glamour... Therefore the paragraph, when pinned to a particular spot, must appear diminished – a fake. And yet it is true.

The facts of Conrad's life are extraordinary enough: self-exiled Pole who becomes a British merchant sea captain, only to transform himself into one of the greatest 'English' novelists of the twentieth century. But Conrad was not averse to glamorising the facts in his attempts to attain a poetic truth. It is not always easy to disentangle the twists in the yarn. Conrad's life is as elusive as his art.

Joseph Conrad was born Jozef Teodor Konrad Korzenowski on 3rd December 1857 at Berdyczow in the Polish Ukraine. Since 1795, Poland had ceased to be an independent state having been carved between Austria, Prussia and Russia. Berdyczow was in Russian territory and Conrad was born a Russian subject, liable, somewhat later, to twenty-five years' military service.

Conrad's parents were both involved in the various movements for political independence. Apollo Korzenowski was a gentleman of the landed class, a *szlachta*. He was a minor poet, a patriot and a man who was both of fixed purpose and yet something of a dreamer. Above all, he was an intellectual, who translated Shakespeare and Hugo to boost this income.

Conrad's mother was of equal social standing. Eva Bobrowski was intelligent, gentle and, by all accounts, something of a saint. Whereas the Korzenowskis had stirred up problems with the Russians, and had been rewarded by having most of their land confiscated, the Bobrowskis were by tradition cautious, hardworking and sensible. They stood aloof from trouble, and were appeasers. This tradition was peddled enthusiastically by Conrad's uncle Tadeusz, and fell some distance short of reality.

Apollo had some difficulty marrying Eva. After all, he had not much to recommend him. There was a twelve-year age gap. In Tadeusz's words he had 'the reputation of being very ugly and sarcastic. In fact he was not beautiful, not very handsome…' Nor did he have much in the way of financial potential. As a result, Eva's father had the neat idea of leading Apollo around the various country estates in the hope that another young girl might catch his eye. It didn't work and the family finally had to accept a son-in-law of dubious reliability.

On the occasion of Conrad's birth, Apollo produced a poem that mingled personal celebration with a strain of lugubrious patriotism:

Bless you, my little son
Be a Pole! Though enemies
May tempt you
With a web of joy
Renounce it all – love your poverty.
Hush, my baby!

Polish political groups split into two at this time. The 'Whites', who were gradualists, felt negotiating with the Tsar would lead to greater liberalisation. They believed in the political process.

Less optimistic were the 'Reds', who were essentially revolutionaries. At the extreme wing would be those who advocated violence. Apollo was centrist, in that he supported, indeed organised, protest. It was the Reds who organised themselves into the secret National Central Committee which eventually proclaimed the famous (and doomed) insurrection on 22nd January 1863. Before that, Apollo had already been arrested on a number of unrelated charges including 'having caused, with others, the disturbances in Modouva Street and in Wedle's cake and coffee shop' and organising a requiem mass for those killed in the demonstrations of 1861. Eva was said to have pinned black cockades on the mourning rioters. Although Apollo denied the charges initially, he agreed to sign a confession to put an end to the dreary rigmarole of the tribunal. Eva was implicated because letters of a suspicious nature had been found in her handwriting.

The Russian authorities undoubtedly suspected Apollo of more than they could prove, or were prepared to make public. As a result, Apollo and Eva were eventually exiled to a remote district of Russia, Volgada. Conrad was four years old.

During the course of that journey, he fell ill. Apollo refused to proceed and his passive resistance was noted disapprovingly by the authorities, who classified his concern for his son as sentimentality. As Apollo later wrote: 'the decision was taken that, as a child is born ultimately to die, the journey was to proceed at once'.

The climate of Volgada was aggressively unhealthy. There were two seasons of the year: 'a white winter and a green winter. The white winter lasted nine and a half months and the green one two and a half.'

Eva and her son soon fell ill. As a result, the family were eventually transferred to the milder climate of Chernikhov, north east of Kiev. Irreparable damage had already been done. Eva was suffering from advanced tuberculosis. On 18th April 1865, Eva died aged thirty-two, leaving Apollo in charge of a chronically sickly seven year old. Later Conrad was to write: 'I can hardly remember her, but judging by what I heard about her... She must have been a woman with uncommon qualities of mind and spirit.'

Apollo fell into depression. Always prone to bouts of mysticism, he lost his sardonic style, replacing it with morbid religiosity: 'I know I have not suffered and never could suffer like our Saviour, but then I am only a human being. I have kept my eyes fixed on the cross and by that means fortified my fainting soul and reeling brain.'

Life for Conrad cannot have been much fun. He found some form of escape and refuge in reading. In Polish and French translation he devoured adventure books, Scott, Fenimore Cooper, Captain Marryat, Dickens and an abridged edition of *Don Quixote*. He also read his father's translations of Hugo's *Toilers of the Sea* and Shakespeare's *Two Gentlemen of Verona*. He immersed himself in the Polish Romantic poets, Mickiewicz and Stowacki. It is difficult to stress sufficiently the effect that this intensive exposure to imaginative literature must have had: although Apollo was well meaning and aware of his responsibilities, from

Conrad's accounts he was also dour company. Even Apollo himself admitted: 'I teach and demand too much and the little one sees nobody except me and burrows deeply into books.' This from a highly literary individual.

Conrad continued to be afflicted with kidney trouble, and there is a mention of 'fits'. Although sent away to various relatives, Conrad's health remained shaky. In the meantime, his father had contracted, and was dying of, tuberculosis.

Apollo, allowed to travel further afield, made plans for a collected edition of Hugo's theatrical works, an edition of his own poems and a long novel about Polish society from 1854 to 1861. He regained something of his old humour when he noted: 'Most of the time I am ready to drop, but I continue to make plans.' Once again, defiance in the face of the inevitable. Apollo evinces the particular kind of heroism that Conrad was to scrutinise throughout his life, whether as a seaman or a writer. Apollo died on 23rd May 1869. Conrad was eleven years old. In his preface to *A Personal Record* he wrote of his father: 'To a man of such strong faith death could not have been an enemy.' The faith was as much political as it was religious.

Apollo's funeral was a grand affair, and evolved into a patriotic ceremony. Conrad walked at the head of the procession: 'I could see again the small boy of that day following a hearse; a space kept clear in which I walked alone, conscious of an enormous following. Half the population had turned out on that fine May afternoon.'

Conrad was now handed over to his mother's brother, Tadeusz. A greater contrast with Apollo would be hard to picture. Tadeusz was undoubtedly a kind man, whose interest in his nephew was unstinting. He was also sententious and, as his letters indicate with unsparing regularity, he had a taste for stating, in emphatic terms, the obvious. An extra ingredient, which must have made him difficult for an adolescent, was a tendency towards self-righteousness, which could harden into moralising despotism. He remained an abiding influence on

Conrad's life and Conrad always spoke of him with respect, if not affection. His first letters to Conrad, after his father's death, set the tone. It is worth bearing in mind that Conrad is twelve when he is being reminded that:

> without a thorough education you will be nothing in this world, you will never be self sufficient... therefore not that which is easy and attractive must be an object for our studies but that which is useful, although sometimes difficult for a man who knows nothing fundamentally, who knows no strengths of character and no endurance, who does not know how to work on his own and guide himself, ceases to be a man and becomes a useless puppet.

These principles read like an awkward summary of Conrad's later novelistic themes.

Not much is known about Conrad's formal education or whether he was able to make much in the way of friends. There are a couple of names, the occasional suggestion of flirtation with a fellow student's sister. He seems to have endured a haphazard mixture of schooling and private tutoring. In later life, Conrad claimed that he was enrolled at St Anne's Gymnasium in Cracow. There are no records of his doing so: clearly he was trying to smooth over yet another difficult kink in his life. In any case, he does not seem to have taken his studies particularly seriously, although he enjoyed geography – and the odd cigar.

It is tempting to make heavy weather of Conrad's decision, sometime in 1872, to go to sea; and few critics and biographers have resisted the temptation. Largely this is Conrad's fault: in later life he was keen to insist that becoming a seaman was part of his fate. He also had to defend himself from the charge of deserting his homeland for the sake of trivial ambition. But the more portentously he defended himself, the less convincing he tended to sound:

Why should I undertake the pursuit of fantastic meals of salt junk and hard tack upon the wide seas? – the part of the inexplicable should be allowed for appraising the conduct of men in a world where no explanation is final.

No single reason can account for the decision, but it is easy to see why the idea, once in place, had attractions for both Conrad and Tadeusz. To begin with, Conrad needed both literal and metaphorical fresh air. He had suffered from the deaths of both his parents and subsequent chronic ill health. A nervy, over sensitive individual, he wanted to escape the clutches of Tadeusz and his mother's family. More simply, with a head stuffed with Scott and Fenimore Cooper and Marryat, he required adventure – and at sixteen, he was unlikely to choose voluntarily a safe career in law or the civil service. Other pressures would include the need to find citizenship in another country to avoid the draft into the Russian army; and the certainty that he would never conform to the Brobowski notion of 'a sane and sensible' life.

As for Tadeusz, a sign of independence on behalf of his nephew was likely to be greeted with quiet enthusiasm. Conrad was obviously a difficult adolescent, vaguely uncooperative, and wholly uncommitted. He also cost the family and Tadeusz (in particular) a lot of money, without much gratitude in return. It is also worth bearing in mind that neither Tadeusz nor Conrad himself can have foreseen that the break would be permanent. Both sides may have believed that the idea would peter out after six months of mucking about in boats.

France
1874–8

In October 1874, not yet seventeen, Conrad left Poland for Marseille. Of course, it may be that Conrad felt some measure of regret at departure, some pang of homesickness; more likely, given his youth, he looked forward to new experiences.

They came aplenty. One of the first people he met in Marseille was Baptistin Solary who had been appointed to look after him. The contrast with Tadeusz and the musty stewardship of his grandmother could not have been more brutal:

> I was still asleep in my room in a modest hold near the quays of the old port, after the fatigues of the journey via Vienna, Zurich, Lyon when he (Baptistin) burst in flinging the shutters open to the sun of Provence and chiding me boisterously for lying abed.

Here was a new world of light and energy and fun. The gloom of the Brobowskis is exchanged for the high octane frolicking of the 'sturdy, Provençal seaman.'

> And many a day and a night, too, did I spend cruising with these rough, kindly men, under whose auspices my intimacy with the sea began... Their sea tanned faces, whiskered or shaved, lean or full, with the intent, wrinkled sea eyes of the pilot breed, and here and there a thin gold hoop at the

lobe of a hairy ear, bent over my sea infancy... And I have been invited to sit in more than one tall, dark house of the old town at their hospitable board, had the bouillabaisse ladled out into a thick plate by their high-voiced broad-browed wives, talked to their daughters – thickset girls, with pure profiles, glorious masses of black hair arranged with complicated art, dark eyes, and dazzling white teeth.

The above passage, from *A Personal Record*, is plumply over-loaded with sensuous detail: the faces of the sailors, the food, the girls, it was almost too much for Conrad. Clearly the elderly author remembers his adolescent self's first introduction to the delights of independence with liberating delight.

It is a relief to imagine Conrad eating, drinking, joking and having sex. Unfortunately, the evidence for what actually occurred in Marseille has to be inferred from the merest trickle of factual information. Conrad himself tended to romanticise this part of his life more than any other, portraying himself as a swashbuckling young privateer involved in gunrunning and underground political activism.

As far as drink and sex are concerned, Conrad showed no signs of excess in either department. There are no witnesses to his being drunk; indeed given that he was a sailor, he showed a tendency, later in life, towards disciplined sobriety. As for sex, Conrad's reticence on this subject makes Henry James seem a vibrant exhibitionist. Apart from his future wife, there is no evidence that he slept with anybody else.

And yet. A photograph taken of him in 1873 shows a striking youth with exotic good looks. The dark hair is swept back, the expression an odd mixture of piercing and dreamy, the whole exuding obtrusive moodiness. It is hard to believe that, away from home, with the temptation of all that black hair and those dazzling teeth, he kept himself to himself.

What is documented is that he was, and remained, hope-less with money. Although he packed himself off to Marseille ostensibly to make a living, Tadeusz supplied him (and kept supplying him) with a hefty allowance of 1000 francs a year. To put this into perspective, for his first job Conrad was paid a monthly salary of 35 francs. For the next few years he overspent but it was not clear, least of all to his uncle, where the money was going. A typical example of Tadeusz's reasonable frustration:

> Perhaps it seems to you that I can bear such extraordinary expenditure out of love for my 'dearly beloved Nephew'? But this is not the case… If I were to give you 300 roubles more per year… I would have to cut down my expenditure on underwear, shoes, clothes and my personal needs… Is it fair that I should repair your thoughtlessness at the expense of my personal comforts or, I should rather say, my essential needs.

Although Conrad could not have felt at ease with himself, the tide of his expenditure rose, with near fatal results. One explanation is that because Conrad saw himself as a *szlachta* he refused to compromise his standards and demanded the best clothes, expensive accommodation, good food and excellent cigars. Even so, it is possible that he also lost money, if not gambling – Tadeusz vigorously denied that Conrad was a gambler – then in rash business ventures.

Within two months of his arrival in Marseille, Conrad set off on his first sea voyage on the *Mont Blanc*, a small barque of 400 tons with a crew of roughly a dozen. Embarking on 8th December the ship sailed for Mustique on the 15th and arrived on 6th February 1875. He was a passenger and was presumably on board to observe, before he became an apprentice. It was either on this voyage or the next, when in port at Saint-Pierre, that Conrad visited (for the only time in his life) the coast of South America (Venezuela and Colombia), the setting for his epic novel *Nostromo*.

It might seem fatuously self-evident to point out that Conrad obviously had an astonishing ear for languages. Although Apollo taught him French from an early age, the French he would have been taught would not have helped him converse with the sailors who were his sole companions on the *Mont Blanc*. The Marseille accent is particularly nasal and impenetrable, the slang incomprehensible.

On his return to Marseille, he continued to spend. The owners of the *Mont Blanc*, Monsieur Delestang, 'a frozen-up mummified Royalist' and his wife, an 'imperious' woman who reminded Conrad of Lady Dedlock in Dickens' *Bleak House*, moved in relatively exalted circles, and Conrad moved with them. He took a break after his seven months at sea, to visit the theatre and the opera. Conrad liked Bizet's *Carmen* and the model of a fiery, sexy Mediterranean beauty was to haunt many of his later attempts to inject old-fashioned 'romance' into his stories.

Yet he seems to have 'got by' even if there must have been hours, if not days, of loneliness and isolation. Through Delestang he also met the forty-two year old Corsican, Dominique Cervoni, who also sailed on Conrad's next ship, the *Saint Antoine*.

Cervoni was charismatic and became the model for the eponymous hero Nostromo:

> In his eyes lurked a look of perfectly remorseless irony, as though he had been provided with an extremely experienced soul; and the slightest distension of the nostrils would give to his bronzed face a look of extraordinary boldness.

It seems possible that Conrad fell under Cervoni's spell, becoming involved in smuggling both in Marseille and off the South American coast. On the other hand, it may be that Cervoni entranced Conrad with romantic stories of gun running and that Conrad appropriated the experiences.

Conrad would later describe how he smuggled arms for the Spanish Pretender to the throne, Don Carlos de Borbon y de

Austria Este. The whole episode is reminiscent of the Jacobite novels of Scott: a young man finds himself in an alien environment, falls in love, dedicates himself to a doomed political cause. Indeed, the Scott model is so close, one is tempted to speculate that Conrad moulded his experiences, whatever they were, accordingly.

Documentary evidence suggests that Conrad's claim to being a Carlist supporter may have been no more than wishful thinking. Marseille police archives give plenty of evidence of Carlist activity prior to 1876, but there are neither files nor newspaper reports for the years 1877–8 when Conrad was lurking around Marseille. What we do know, is that he was unable to complete a second voyage on the *Saint Antoine* because of an anal abscess.

If that wasn't sufficient, he also had to endure a bureaucratic confusion with his papers. He had failed to secure from the Russian council permission to work on board ship.

This period of Conrad's life is lightly documented but also lavishly fictionalised by Conrad himself. In *The Arrow of Gold* the hero has a passionate affair with Rita de Lastaola, who some have presumed must have existed in one form or another. If there was a love affair at this time, Rita herself can give no idea who the mystery woman might have been. One of Conrad's poorer creations, she is a Carmen fantasy who lacks only castanets as she smoulders her way through the novel. Any attempts to identify her with a real person can only be guesswork.

However, one can piece together a possible narrative: Conrad finds himself yet again in horrendous debt; his future appears uncertain; he is unlucky in love; his uncle is exerting the usual pressure; he feels lonely, probably physically unwell, certainly depressed. Out of this rich emotional stew, Conrad takes the romantic escape route that had been the popular option since the publication of Goethe's masterpiece of self-indulgent melancholy, *Werther*: he attempts suicide.

Not that he was ever to admit it. Even when a comparatively old man, showing his son John the scars, he would adhere to the tale that he had engaged in a duel: cutlasses, the lot. If there was a duel, there were no witnesses, no accomplices, no known fellow duellist. The fiction ties neatly in with Conrad's glamorous promotion of his youthful self, but doesn't square with the letter that Tadeusz Brobowski wrote to Stefan Buszeynki, an old friend of Conrad's father:

I was quite sure he was somewhere in the Antipodes when, suddenly, while engaged in business at the Kiev Fair in 1878, I received a telegram reading: 'Conrad blesse envoyez argent – arrivez' [Conrad wounded, send money, come]... On arrival, I found that Conrad was already able to walk and, after a previous talk with his friend Mr Richard Fecht... I visited the delinquent. This is what happened... the Bureau de l'Inscription forbade [Conrad's sailing] as he was an alien, aged 21 and liable to military service in his country [Russia]. Moreover it came out that Conrad had never received permission from his consul, so that the former Inspector of the Port of Marseilles was summoned to explain why he had noted on the list that such permission had been granted. He was reprimanded and very nearly lost his post... Conrad had to stay ashore without hope of serving as a seaman in French vessels. Before all this happened, however, another catastrophe, a financial one overtook him...

Tadeusz goes on to mention Conrad's possible involvement in some dubious affair off the coast of Spain – and his wishing 'to repair his finances; by losing 800 francs at the gaming tables in Monte Carlo'. Tadeusz continued to assert that his nephew was not a gambler:

Having so excellently managed his affairs, he invited the aforesaid friend (Richard Fecht) to tea; but before the time fixed he attempted to kill himself with a revolver shot. (Let this detail remain between us; for I have told everyone that he was wounded in a duel. But I do not want to keep this a secret from you.) The bullet went durch and durch [through and through] near the heart, not injuring any important organ. Luckily he had left all his addresses on top so that good Mr Fecht could immediately notify me and even my brother who, again, bombarded me in turn. That is the whole story.

Conrad's invitation to his friend suggested that he wanted to be found; had he wanted to shoot himself and be certain of the outcome, a bullet to the head would surely have ensured a positive result.

Of course, Conrad was desperate. Again and again, he was to return to suicide in his novels; not as a means of escape, but as a final gesture of exhaustion: 'Suicide is very often the outcome of mere mental weakness – not an act of savage energy but the final symptom of complete collapse.'

Another possible explanation for Conrad's state of mind is embedded in his sense of honour. Conrad must have felt ashamed that his Marseille adventure, starting so propitiously, had fizzled out in debt and unemployment. Throughout his life, he carried with him the demeanour of a (minor) aristocrat and wanted to live up to an ideal conception of himself. To have failed so publicly, involving as he did the Marseille officials, would have been a torment to an individual of Conrad's sensitive and self-aware temperament. In *Lord Jim*, he was to explore shame and its complex emotional ramifications with forensic enthusiasm.

Tadeusz rescued his nephew, as he was to do many times in the future. He paid the debts, tidied the mess, and set about making suggestions for Conrad's future.

For a prospective sailor, Conrad was burning more boats than might be thought wise. Tadeusz had worried over Conrad's citizenship before: the spectre of Russian military service still hovered over the twenty-one year old. Switzerland had been suggested, but this was hardly going to give much of a boost to Conrad's career on the high seas.

Conrad would have to move on. Apart from the fact that he was unemployable, there might well be a romantic complication, unresolved, lurking in the back streets or boudoirs of Marseille. Becoming a British merchant seaman provided a possible solution. Conrad, in later years, was to play up the fact that this was the obvious step, given the self-evident splendour of the British Merchant Navy. Perhaps so. On the other hand, the British authorities were also less fussy about paperwork and would accept him for work without having to clear the matter with the Russians.

England and the Merchant Service
1878–89

On 24th April 1878 he boarded the *Mavis* which was bound for Constantinople with a cargo of coal; and on 18th June, Conrad reached England, docking at Lowestoft. It is a wonder that he coped without any sort of fluent English. It has been mooted that he was entirely without English, but this is difficult to believe. He must have been able to understand simple instructions, and make some sort of reply, if nothing more.

It is heartening to note that Conrad was as awkward as ever. He had a row with the captain of the *Mavis*, blew his money in London, and earned for his pains a long tirade from Tadeusz with the usual accusations of recklessness, of being a 'lazybones' and a 'spendthrift'. Perhaps only those who constitutionally evade duty and responsibility can appreciate what those words really mean. In any event, Conrad found himself a berth on *The Skimmer of the Sea* carrying coals from Newcastle to Lowestoft. At this point, he begins his career in earnest, leading the tough life of an ordinary seaman: 'I began to learn English from East Coast chaps each built as though to last forever and coloured like a Christmas card.'

In later life, he was to claim that he learned English from newspapers, with a dash of Shakespeare thrown in to leaven the mixture. After seventy-three days on the *Skimmer* he moved to London seeking further work:

No explorer could have been more lonely. I did not know a single soul of all these millions that all around me peopled the mysterious distances of the streets.

On 12th October he embarked on the *Duke of Sutherland*, a wool clipper with a crew of twenty-three, bound for Australia.

It is difficult to exaggerate the physical and psychological hardships of life as an ordinary seaman in the Merchant Service in 1878. A sailor's day was twelve hours, divided into seven watches (when sailors could not converse) round the clock. When not 'on watch', the sailors had time to repair clothes and rest, but only if weather conditions were fine. The food was poor, with due emphasis on salted meat.

They had to wash down decks, clean masts, repair sails, steer. The crew's quarters also needed looking after. The drudgery and boredom was incessant: on the other hand, Conrad must have found the routine and clarity of relationships on a ship comforting. For an exiled individual, perplexed by his own sense of identity, the straightforward lines of command would come as a relief. Conversely the lack of privacy and cramped living conditions were oppressive. It is doubtful that Tadeusz ever understood what his nephew had let himself in for.

The usual way of presenting Conrad's progress through the Merchant Navy is to view it as one unalloyed triumph after another: Conrad was certainly keen for it to be regarded in this flattering light. The truth is more interesting. When Conrad applied for his second mate's ticket in 1880 – he had already had enough of the rollicking life of an ordinary seaman – he indulged in a spot of fraud. To become a second mate in the British Merchant Service, you needed to have served a total of four years at sea. Conrad had managed nothing like that. Still, with the help of Delestang, his employer in Marseille, he composed a fictive French career for himself, stretching his thirteen months and five days of service into three years. If nothing else, Conrad was ambitious.

He passed the exam and was awarded his certificate. To have done so, Conrad would have had to be proficient in English, able to read and write with sufficient command to fulfil his new status as an officer, and show himself worthy of earning over three pounds a month. However, even as he was dedicating himself to seafaring, he was also considering taking up the post of secretary with a Mr Lascalle, a Canadian businessman. Throughout his life, Conrad was both determined yet willing to experiment with different possibilities for himself, long before he settled on becoming a 'great' novelist.

In the meantime, he was still cadging off Tadeusz. One particularly bizarre episode involves Conrad claiming he had lost all his kit with the wrecking of the *Anna Frost*, and asking Tadeusz for a loan of ten pounds. There is no record of an *Anna Frost*: the *Annie Frost* was engaged on a voyage round the world, but there is no record of Conrad as a crewmember. The ship completed its voyage.

On 19th September 1881 Conrad found a birth on the *Valentine* under a Captain Beard. Neither ship nor captain would inspire confidence, both having been subject to wear and tear.

This proved to be a genuinely disastrous experience which Conrad turned to good copy in his short story 'Youth'. Although much of Conrad's early fiction – like that of most novelists – is rooted in what he saw and whom he met, it is never just a question of his recording events. In his 'Author's Notes' he often emphasised the documentary material, in order to defend himself from the charge of exaggeration. In doing so, he has encouraged biographers to hunt for the 'real' people behind fictional types. This has not always led to a finer appreciation of his writing.

'Youth' is the exception. He does give quite a crisp and no doubt accurate account of the voyage, without too much gingering up of the material: poor old Captain Beard remains, in the story, Captain Beard. But, as we have seen, the end was glamorised, so that the East is virtually personified as a perfumed seductress. The rest of the story adheres closely enough to facts: the *Palestine* had difficulties leaving Falmouth, but when finally ready, sailed to Java, without a hitch, until the coal self-ignited and blew up the decks 'fore and aft' as 'far as the poop'. The ship went down. In the story, understandably enough, Conrad assigned his youthful alter ego Marlow with a heroic role, steering an open boat for days on the unfriendly sea. The truth was that Conrad took only a few hours to reach shore. No doubt it did not feel that way. In the story, Conrad wants to link his first sighting of the East with the onset of his maturity: he was twenty-five. The chief mate Mahon described him as 'an excellent fellow, good officer, the best second mate I ever sailed with'.

Even so, Conrad frequently quarrelled with those who were nominally in charge of him. Though he despised revolutionaries, he remained something of a rebel all his life. The dandified teenager who strutted the quays of Marseille still resided in the stout heart of the polite and thoughtful merchant officer. He was sacked from his next ship, the *Riverdale*, for accusing the captain of being a drunk. Conrad was compelled to write an apology and pay sixty rupees in compensation. One can imagine Conrad's reaction when he learned that the *Riverdale* ran aground off the coast, in fine weather, twenty-four hours after leaving port. The captain had his licence revoked for a year: perhaps Conrad had mistaken inebriation for plain incompetence.

Conrad was visited with further bad luck when he returned from Bombay on the *Narcissus*, the experience which furnished material for his masterpiece, *The Nigger of the Narcissus*. He also brought back to England a monkey (for company?), which caused him no end of trouble until he disposed of it 'in the Minories'.

There were further voyages out East, in the *Tilkurst* and the *Highland Forest*, as well as more exams to take and pass.

The chief mate's and the master's certificates required know-ledge of seamanship, stowing, rigging, navigation and nautical astronomy. Conrad would be expected to know how to find latitude using a star, how best to pack coal, how to prevent disease aboard ship. Conrad did not take the extra master's exams, which involved knowledge of trigonometry. Tough though all this sounds, the French equivalents were even more demanding.

Edward Blackmore noted in *The British Mercantile Mariner* (1897) that 'In the standard of education as proved by examinations we are far behind those other nations whose example we professed to follow...' The natural superiority of the British Merchant Service was not self-evident, despite Conrad's testimony to the contrary. After a couple of hiccoughs, Conrad qualified as chief mate, and eventually as master. Jobs though were as hard to find as ever, and he still relied on a hefty allowance from Tadeusz. Finally, on 19th August 1886, Conrad acquired British citizenship.

Once again, he stretched the truth: he claims that he was twelve years old when he left Russia, had spent ten years as a British merchant seaman, and held an appointment as chief mate. In fact, he was ten years old when he went to Lwow (possibly a genuine mistake), had served eight years in the Service, and, up to that point, had not been given a job as chief mate. It is understandable that he should massage one or two details to achieve his aim, but it is odd that he was prepared to endanger his citizenship in this way. No doubt he was relying on the laziness of the officials, which he must have regarded as a sine qua non.

In 1887 Conrad left for the East on a final visit, as first mate aboard the *Highland Forest*, an iron barque of 1,040 tons with a crew of eighteen. He was later to be remembered with affection. One of his crew members wrote:

He was exceedingly kind to us boys, a thing that is not easily forgotten... we, like most boys at the age when I was under Mr Conrad, did not realise what kindness really meant.

On this trip Conrad appears to have fallen ill and, as ever, Tadeusz provided his nephew with financial assistance once he arrived at Semerang. For the next four months, Conrad's movements are difficult to track, although he was in hospital for a spell. Now he was able to observe colonialism at close quarters. The Dutch emerged as a dominant force in the Malay Archipelago after a series of conflicts in 1623. They retained a hold on the territories, despite continued British interest. Although by the late nineteenth century they were supposed to be ruling indirectly through local sultans and chiefs, they continued to interfere directly in the internal affairs of the states for their own profit. The native population suffered social dislocation without any economic advantage. Years later, Conrad noted with asperity that the Boers 'have no idea of liberty, which can only be found under the British flag all over the world. C'est un peuple essentiellement despotique, like by the way all the Dutch.'

It was whilst serving as chief mate on the *Vidar*, his next ship, that Conrad met Charles William Olmeijer who was to become the protagonist of Conrad's first novel *Almayer's Folly*. The *Vidar* left Singapore, calling at Borneo, Pulau Laut, the Celebes and back again, transporting coal. The voyage was comparatively leisurely, with Conrad recovering from his illness. Olmeijer, when Conrad met him, was married to a fellow Eurasian and had eleven children; because he has few outward similarities to the white Almayer and his single daughter, critics tend to ignore Conrad's statement in *A Personal Record* that: 'if I had not got to know Almayer pretty well it is almost certain there would never have been a line of mine in print!'

But something about him and his remote location at Tanjung Redeb inspired Conrad to reflect on individuals who, cut off from the commonplace habits of civilisation, find themselves drawn further into a world of baseless hope and predictable self-delusion. The fact that Conrad was able to marry these observations to the insights of his favourite authors Flaubert and Maupassant, must have added piquancy to the brew. Two years after taking up his berth on the *Vidar*, Conrad began his first novel in earnest, though it is possible that he was sketching ideas earlier. After all, it was a long slow haul on the *Vidar*, and there must have been gaps of time that needed filling. (At the opening of *Lord Jim*, Conrad disapproves of sailors who renounce storms and hard work for 'the peace of Eastern sky and sea', loving 'short passages, good deck chairs, large native crews and the distinction of being white'.)

On 9th January 1888 Conrad left Singapore for Bangkok to take over command of the 346-ton iron sailing barque, *Otago*. This was to be the only time that he was to be master of his own ship. He was replacing John Snadden who had died whilst in charge: a slightly odd character, he had spent much of his time locked in his cabin, playing the violin. In *The Shadow-Line*, Conrad's fictional reinterpretation of this voyage, he is also supposed to have flogged the medical supplies as well. Though not impossible, this was unlikely to have been the case.

The master of a ship had both full responsibility and exclusive authority for all that took place. He could have little in the way of companionship and the role was wedded to loneliness. On the other hand, this was a small crew of nine (captain, two officers, six sailors), so one must avoid becoming overdramatic. On 3rd March, the *Otago* finally left port for Sydney. On his arrival, two months later, Conrad agreed to stay in charge.

The next voyage, laden with fertiliser, soap and tallow, was for Mauritius. Despite having twice failed his navigation exams Conrad had the bright idea of tackling the more difficult route, by way of the Torres Strait. Although this is a long way round, it is supposed to be quicker: in fact it did not prove particularly fast, fifty-four days.

The *Otago* docked in Port Louis in Mauritius on 30th September. One of the ship's charters there describes Conrad as he appeared at thirty-one:

Captain Korzeniowski was always dressed with great elegance. I can still see him... arriving in my office almost every day dressed in a black or dark coat, a vest that was usually light in colour and fancy trousers; everything well cut and very stylish; on his head a black and grey derby tilted slightly to one side. He invariably wore gloves and carried a cane with a gold knob... He was not... very popular with his colleagues, who sarcastically called him 'the Russian Count'.

Apart from giving some idea about how Conrad spent his money, the passage also shows that he still saw himself as a Polish noble-man – *szlachta* to the tips of his elegant gloves. Conversely, it is not difficult to detect in this account an underlying pulse of xeno-phobia and racism. Poles and Russians are all the same: foreign and untrustworthy.

Although Conrad must have known he was the victim of gibes of this sort he gives no sign in his fiction, or elsewhere, that he took offence. He managed to tread a subtle line, asserting his Polishness through dress and demeanour whilst apologising for his accent and acknowledging his idiosyncratic ways. As a result, Conrad exuded an exotic charm.

Gabriel Renouf, a captain in the Merchant Navy, had intro-duced him to the household of Louis Schmidt. It was there that Conrad took a fancy to Eugenie Renouf. Schmidt's sister-in-law, she in her turn clearly found Conrad unusual and provoking. An 'Album de Confidences' shows that, as part of a party game, the elusive Polish captain had been forced to answer a question-naire. Although he would have spoken to the family in French, his replies were in English. Some of Conrad's answers are sur-prisingly revealing:

What is your chief character trait? – Laziness.
How do you amuse yourself – By making myself scarce.
What is your dream of happiness? – Never dream of it; want reality.

What would you like? – Should like not to be.

In which country would you like to live? – Do not know. Perhaps Lapland.

What do you most dislike? – False pretences.

Of course, Conrad is keen on irony and he is literally playing a game here. Even so the mixture of sharp introspection and temperamental gloom comes across noisily, just as it does in his fiction. And without the wishing to make heavy weather of it, a fear of laziness was to haunt Conrad for much of his life.

Shortly before he was due to sail Conrad declared his wish to marry Eugenie, only to discover she was betrothed already, to a pharmacist. For the remaining two days of his time in Mauritius he stayed aboard ship. The incident was later transformed in the story 'A Smile of Fortune', where a young captain flirts with the daughter of a ship chandler in a garden which was 'a brilliantly coloured solitude, drowsing in a warm voluptuous silence'.

On 22nd November the *Otago* sailed for Melbourne. After further brief voyages, Conrad resigned his command. A romantic explanation is that the owners wanted him to return to Port Louis but that Conrad was not keen on revisiting the scene of his humiliation. Another theory is that he got sick of pootling around the Australian coast and wanted to strike out for Africa. Most likely, Conrad was sick of looking after a small ship and wanted to return to Europe, perhaps with the notion of starting a new career. Certainly the owners of the *Otago* take that line: 'we now have much pleasure in stating that this early severance from our employ is entirely at your own desire, with a view to visiting Europe...' On his arrival in London, he rented rooms in Pimlico.

Conrad's progress as a merchant seaman had been chequered. Although he was usually popular with his crew and had earned the respect of ship owners, he had never been given command of a large vessel. He had tended to serve on small ships and would quit for no 'good' reason, as in the case of the *Otago*.

Tadeusz's allowance gave him freedom in this respect, but may also have proven something of a career hindrance. Conrad was by temperament nervous, fidgety and easily bored.

When he began *Almayer's Folly*, he claims that it was by accident:

> The conception of a planned book was entirely outside my mental range when I sat down to write; the ambition of being an author had never turned up amongst these gracious imaginary existences one creates fondly for oneself...

In 1903 he wrote to an old Polish friend: 'I began writing Almayer's Folly just like that, not thinking much what I was doing in order to occupy my mornings during a rather long stay in London after a three years' cruise in the South Seas.'

The Apprentice Writer
1889–95

Why did Conrad choose to write in English? There is no pat answer. His own response was simple. He had been thinking in English for years, he loved the language and it never occurred to him to write in either Polish or French. Besides, the Polish novel was, in 1889, still in its infancy. Psychologically, it may have been appealing to Conrad to master a craft. In the early stages of his career as a sailor, he did not find it easy and this may have been the point. Fearing the charge of laziness, he wanted to prove to himself that he could overcome the intricacies of English grammar and vocabulary – rather like choosing the most difficult sailing route. And it is possible that writing in English gave him 'distance' from his subject matter: whilst consciously engaged in the manipulation of sentences, the complicated unconscious stuff would bubble to the surface without undue self-consciousness. In any case, Conrad was to carry round with him the manuscript of his first novel for the next five years.

On 24th September 1889, Captain Thys, acting manager of the Société Anonyme Belge pour le Commerce du Haut Congo in Brussels, asked Conrad's broker whether he could possibly employ Conrad in the Congo: 'his general education is superior to that of most seamen and he is a perfect gentleman.' Conrad was to admit that Africa had always seemed to him a seductive possibility and, interviewed in November, he was appointed the following April. This was to prove the most momentous journey of his life.

In the meantime, he visited his uncle in Poland, striking up an unusual relationship with a Madame Poradowska, a beautiful intellectual novelist whom Conrad called 'aunt'. She was six years older than him, but Tadeusz certainly saw her as a threat to Conrad's celibate condition. It is interesting that Conrad was still being protected by Tadeusz, even though he was now in his early thirties. It was on this visit that his uncle handed to Conrad the Document, with a full financial account of his upbringing. 'Thus the making of a man out of Mr Konrad has cost – apart from the 3,600 roubles given you as capital – 17,454 roubles.'

When Conrad returned to England, there was an opening in the Congo after a steamer captain, Freiseleben, had been murdered at Tchumbiri. Three months after his death he was still unburied and a missionary noted that 'the hair is cut off and made into a fringe and tied around his face.'

There is little doubt that Conrad was quite unprepared for what he was about to encounter. The Congo was the private property of Leopold II, King of the Belgians. He had promoted the 'International Association for the Suppression of Slavery and the Opening Up of Central Africa' in 1876. At its first conference he announced that he was prepared 'To open to civilisation the only area of our globe to which it has not penetrated, to pierce the gloom which hangs over entire races', all in the name of progress. In 1885 Leopold was internationally recognised as sovereign of the International State of the Congo. Underneath the propaganda, Leopold was indulging in ruthless economic exploitation, slavery and murder. Possibly eight to ten million people died under Leopold's careful stewardship. Conrad signed a three-year contract, taking the manuscript of *Almayer's Folly* with him, in case he found time on his hands.

After a month's journey, Conrad reached Bonna and from there he steamed up to Matadi where he met Roger Casement, whom Conrad found 'most intelligent and very sympathetic'.

Casement was good-looking, idealistic and Conrad fell under his spell:

> He's a Protestant Irishman, pious too... there is a touch of the Conquistador in him too; for I've seen him start off into an unspeakable wilderness... with two bulldogs... at his heels and a Land boy carrying a bundle for all company. A few months afterwards I saw him come out a little leaner, a little browner... quietly serene as though he had been for a stroll in the park.

Casement was employed as a supervisor of the projected railway line from Matadi to Leopoldville. In 1903, he was to be instrumental in bringing to light some of the horrors of Leopold's Congo in which torture and mutilation were regarded as commonplace management devices. He may well have alerted Conrad to expect unpleasantness up river.

Although *Heart of Darkness*, the masterpiece that emerged from Conrad's journey, was once reckoned an exaggeration, latterly it has been viewed as surprisingly accurate. Men were chained together, workers were paid in brass rods, cannibalism was not unknown; for the merchant seaman, used to order and routine, the environment would have been alien beyond belief.

There was an eighteen days' march between Matadi and Kinshasa. Conrad kept a brief diary (in English) which is laconic in the extreme: 'Met an officer of the State inspecting. A few minutes afterwards saw at a camping place the dead body of a Backongo. Shot. Horrid smell.' The following day he observes: 'another dead body lying by the path in an attitude of meditative repose'.

At Kinshasa, he fell out with his superior Camille Delacommune: 'The manager is a common ivory dealer with sordid instincts who considers himself a merchant, though he is only a kind of African shopkeeper.'

Conrad made only one trip up river, a thousand miles to the Stanley Falls in a 'tin-pot steamer', the *Roi des Belges*. Initially, it was commanded by Ludwig Koch, a young Dane. The crew of thirty included one or two cannibals. Tadeusz joked: 'I feel confident that sooner or later I shall hear from you, provided that you have not been already cooked and eaten as a roast.'

Whatever Casement may have told him, Conrad was able to see for himself the destructive effects of the Belgian administration. On 1st September 1890, after a month's journey, Conrad reached the Falls. Five days later Koch fell ill, and Conrad found himself in charge. Although the journey may not have been as terrifying as it is portrayed in *Heart of Darkness*, it would have been grim enough.

At Stanley Falls, instead of the exotic adventure of his boyhood dreams, he found the pulsing heart of Leopold's ruthless capitalist enterprise.

On 7th September, he set off to return to Kinshasa. On board was George-Antoine Klein, a recently appointed agent, who was suffering from dysentery. He died on the 21st and his name is to be found in the draft of *Heart of Darkness*, before Conrad hit on Kurtz. He bore no similarity to his fictional counterpart, who was more likely to have been based on the model of Faust. It is also possible that Conrad may have heard of the later exploits of Leon Rom, who was living in Leopoldville in the 1890s. When he was station chief of Stanley Falls in 1895, a British journalist noted that, in a recent military expedition: 'Many women and children were taken, and twenty-one heads were brought to the falls and have been used by Captain Rom as a decoration round the flower-beds in front of the house.'

Conrad also fell ill with dysentery and malaria. The *Roi des Belges* reached Kinshasa on 24th September, but Conrad was in no fit state to continue his work, and he now had a decent excuse to break his contract. He had spent only six months in Africa, but he had seen enough. A witness wrote: 'I am in company with… captain Conrad from the Kinshasha company: he is continually sick with dysentery and fever.' He was later to tell Edward Garnett, his friend and publisher: 'before the Congo I was a perfect animal… I see everything with such despondency – all in black.'

On 1st February 1891, he finally returned to London where two of his old friends Hope and Krieger saw to it that he went to hospital. G.F. Hope was a businessman, whom Conrad had met through sailing agents; Adolf Krieger was a partner in a firm of shipping agents. Both were shocked by what they saw. Visiting Conrad in hospital, Hope later wrote that: 'the Nurse said she thought he would die, but he pulled round and in a few weeks was able to go to his rooms, Gillingham Street, near Victoria Station.' Conrad's resilience was not to be underestimated.

For the next few months he scouted around, looking for work, without success. His letters to the stately Madame Poradowska are replete with pessimism: 'I am still plunged in deepest night, and my dreams are only nightmares.' This was to be followed by: 'This evening I feel as if I were in a corner, spine broken, nose in the dust.'

Conrad was always depressive and the Congo experience exacerbated this to the point where he seems clinically ill. On the other hand, one must be careful not to go too far down this route: during all this time, he was still working on *Almayer's Folly*, still capable of focusing his mind on the difficult task of writing an entirely original novel in a foreign language.

Sickness came and went, but eventually, on 14th November, Conrad felt strong enough to accept the berth of first mate in the passenger clipper *Torrens* (1,334 tons) at a grand salary of £8 a month. On the 25th she left Plymouth for Australia.

The *Torrens* was one of the most famous ships of her time, and one of the very fastest, a favourite for the passage to Adelaide. Without doubt, this was to be Conrad's most prestigious appointment.

He made several voyages to Adelaide. In *A Personal Record* he describes showing *Almayer's Folly* to one of the passengers, a young man just down from Cambridge:

'Well what do you say?' I asked at last. 'Is it worth finishing?'
'Distinctly' he answered in his sedate veiled voice, and then coughed a little.

Conrad understood the cough to be a positive sign.

On the return journey, Conrad made his first contact with a literary figure. John Galsworthy had yet to start his writing career, which was to climax in his being awarded the Nobel Prize.

Galsworthy was a public school, Oxford-educated Englishman who seemed on course to become a solicitor, like his father. Robustly unimaginative, he still had a yen for arty experiences. In a letter to a lady friend, he opined: 'I always want to get inside beautiful things and feel more in touch with them... I wonder if you have the feeling too.' He continues to opine: 'I do wish I had the gift of writing, I really think that is the nicest way of making money going...'

It may be that Galsworthy's innocent cast of mind appealed to Conrad. In his second letter from the *Torrens*, the future Nobel laureate wrote:

The first mate is a Pole called Conrad and is a capital chap, though queer to look at; he is a man of travel and experience in many parts of the world, and has a fund of yarns on which I draw freely. He has been right up the Congo and all around Malacca and Borneo... to say nothing of a little smuggling in the days of his youth...

Galsworthy's grasp of the superficial remains exemplary. In truth, Conrad was growing weary of life travelling the seas with its 'uniform grey of existence'.

Yet again, just as Conrad seemed settled, he jumped ship. The captain of the *Torrens* resigned, and Conrad decided that there was little chance of succeeding him, even if he had so wished. In August 1893, he decided to pay Tadeusz a visit in the Ukraine. This was to be their final meeting; Tadeusz had not much longer to live. Predictably enough, Conrad himself was ill, and he admitted that: 'my uncle looks after me like a boy.' Down the years the relationship remained unchanged.

In September 1893, Conrad managed to find a berth as second mate on the 2,097-ton steamer *Adouwa*. Since his return from the Congo, he was conspicuously moving down the ranks.

On 4th December, the *Adouwa* docked at Rouen; and stayed there. The expected passengers who were to be taken to Quebec never materialised. With nothing better to do, Conrad wrote and revised the tenth chapter of *Almayer's Folly*. Eventually, the *Adouwa* returned to London and Conrad disembarked on 17th January. He did not realise that his career as a merchant seaman had drawn to a muffled close.

From the moment he left Cracow in 1874 until the day he left the *Adouwa*, Conrad had worked in ships for eleven years and two months, spending just over eight years on the water. He had served eight months as third officer, almost four years as second officer, just over two years as first mate and captain for one year and two months. He had worked only nine months on steamers. His skills were honed for sail, and sailing ships were fast disappearing.

Although Conrad romanticised the solidarity of the Merchant Service, there is little doubt that the routine, and the strict discipline of life on board ship, did have its consolations for him. Given his naturally gloomy disposition, the need to be strictly practical, and to follow orders would come as a relief.

But much of the time, he must have been bored and uncomfortable. Ford Madox Ford later emphasised these aspects of Conrad's career with genuine insight:

Conrad's whole existence was passed in a series of ninety day passages, in labouring ships, beneath appalling weathers, amongst duties and work too heavy, in continual discomfort and acute physical pain – with, in between each voyage, a few days spent as Jack-ashore.

Tadeusz died on 10th February 1894. Conrad wrote of him, ten years later: 'I saw him four times during the thirty years of my wanderings but even so I attribute to his devotion, care and influence whatever good qualities I may possess.'

Without doubt, Tadeusz had been tiresomely self-righteous, but he had also been kind and thoughtful. He had looked after his nephew financially and the legacy of 15,000 roubles that he left at his death, enabled Conrad to strike out as a professional novelist.

Freudians might argue that the death of this substitute father figure enabled Conrad to finish his novel. Possibly, possibly not. On 24th April, Conrad wrote to Madame Poradowska:

It is with great sorrow that I have to inform you of the death of Mr Kaspar Almayer which occurred this morning at three o'clock. It's over!... all those people who have spoken into my ear, moved before my eyes... became a crowd of phantoms, who are growing distant dim and indistinct, fading away with the sunlight of this brilliant and sombre day.

In July, the manuscript was sent off to the publishing house of Fischer Unwin. It found its way into the hands of Edward Garnett whose discoveries included D.H. Lawrence. On his recommendation the novel was accepted.

He later wrote of his first meeting with Conrad:

My memory is of seeing a dark-haired man, short but extremely graceful in his nervous gestures, with brilliant eyes, now narrowed and penetrating, now soft and warm, with a manner yet caressing, whose speech was ingratiating, guarded and brusque by turn. I had never before seen a man as masculinely keen yet so femininely sensitive.

(Conrad always maintained it was because of Garnett's encouragement and praise that he went on to write a second novel.) He was to be paid £20 and the novel was published on 29th April 1895.

The Professional Novelist
1895–1903

Although *Almayer's Folly* is a first effort, it is not apprentice work. Conrad had studied Flaubert, Maupassant and Balzac with assiduous care. He had worked on the manuscript for over five years. He had stumbled upon subject matter that was entirely original. From the opening sentences, even the least astute reader might conclude that they are in the presence of a writer blessed with astonishing ability:

> One of those drifting trees grounded on the shelving shore, just by the house, and Almayer, neglecting his dream, watched it with languid interest. The tree swung slowly round, amid the hiss and foam of the water, and soon getting free of the obstruction began to move down stream again, rolling slowly over, raising upwards a long, denuded branch, like a hand lifted in mute appeal to heaven against the river's brutal and unnecessary violence.

All the hallmarks of Conrad's mature fiction, both thematic and stylistic, are stamped on the opening pages. The alienation of the individual, the uncaring brutality of the natural world, the serpentine sentences which begin with close observation and finish with a flourish of dark rhetoric.

Almayer is a Dutch trader in a remote Malay outpost. He hopes that he will soon be able to leave his native wife and take his daughter to Europe where his life will change in all respects. His plans collapse. His daughter betrays him and runs away with a local prince. The discovery of her plan breaks his heart:

> 'I will never forgive you Nina!' he shouted, leaping up madly in the sudden fear of his dream.
>
> This was the last time in his life that he was heard to raise his voice. Henceforth he spoke always in a monotonous whisper like an instrument of which all the strings, but one, are broken in a last ringing clamour under a heavy blow.

Almayer's life, with its mixture of boredom and fantasy, is reminiscent of Madame Bovary's but there is more than an element of the distraught Brabantio in his fate. Conrad's first reading was Shakespeare, and *Othello* provides a tacit inspiration for important elements of the novel.

Along with Kipling, Conrad had now shifted the English novel out of its class-ridden, vicarage-centred complacencies and into entirely new territory, and this was recognised by contemporary reviewers who took time and patience to give the book its due. The *Weekly Sun* chose it for Book of the Week: 'the world will know that a new great, a new splendid region of *Romance* has entered into our literature.' Conrad goes on to be hailed as a writer of genius.

Writing a little later, the reviewer of the *Speaker* is more moderate but equally encouraging:

> The Press has already given utterance to very favourable criticisms on the new story by a new writer called *Almayer's Folly* and it only remains for us to join in the expression of the hope that this may not be the last work from the same pen.

The critical reception might have led Conrad to believe that he had a potential 'bestseller' on his hands; if so, he must have been as disillusioned as Almayer himself. The first impression was of 2,000 copies, and it took seven years before a third impression was required.

Another pattern was falling into place, as Conrad was to face repeatedly the frustrating mixture of critical esteem and popular neglect.

It was at this time that he began courting Jessie George. He had been seeing her since November 1894, and although he interrupted his courtship to flirt once more with Marguerite Poradowska, and perhaps try his luck with a twenty year old French woman, Emilie Briquel, he finally proposed to Jessie early in 1895.

He met her through his friend G.F. Hope. When they married in March she was twenty-two, Conrad thirty-eight. According to Jessie Conrad had asked her to marry him in the National Gallery, as they were sheltering from the rain. In the middle of some inconsequential exchange, he blurted out: 'Look here, my dear, we had better get married at once and get over to France. How soon can you be ready? In a week – a fortnight?' To make himself appear even more appealing, he also told her that a) he had no intention of having children, and b) that he had not long to live.

Some of Conrad's contemporaries and most of his biographers tend to give Jessie George a hard time. The fact that she was a typist is held against her, as is her lack of intellectual engagement. In later life, the fact that she put on weight is regarded as proof of her silly self-indulgence. Conrad should have married some sort of Edwardian Simone de Beauvoir, and he let everyone down by marrying instead a woman who understood his moods, and knew how to withstand his erratic outbursts of temper. It is difficult to grasp the inner workings of any marriage, but by any externally observed criteria the Conrad marriage was to prove successful.

In truth, Conrad needed somebody to look after him, especially after the death of Tadeusz. Although a part of him was fiercely independent, he needed to feel cared for; mothered even. He instinctively grasped that Jessie would fulfil this role. Her family was difficult and argumentative, and she reacted by becoming aggressively placid: a technique that was to hold her in good stead when dealing with Conrad. And as her memoirs make clear, Conrad required tactful handling much of the time. The fact that some of Conrad's literary friends looked down on her in a snobbish and hyper-critical fashion does them little credit, and reinforces the commonly held view that to be an intellectual, you do not have to be endowed with much intelligence.

On the marriage certificate Conrad still described himself as a Master Mariner even though, a few days earlier, his second novel, *An Outcast of the Islands*, had been published.

An Outcast was written relatively rapidly, developing some of the characters and themes of *Almayer*. Often seen as a retread of the earlier novel, it is sharper and wittier. Conrad's bleak sense of fun is seldom given its due. The anti-hero Willems lives with his Malay wife and disreputable family:

> They were a half-caste, lazy lot, and he saw them as they were – ragged, lean, unwashed, undersized men of various ages, shuffling about aimlessly in slippers; motionless old women who looked like monstrous bags of pink calico stuffed with shapeless lumps of fat, and deposited askew upon decaying rattan chairs in shady corners of dusty verandahs; young women, slim and yellow, big-eyed, long haired, moving languidly amongst the dirt and rubbish of their dwellings as if every step they took was going to be their very last. He heard their shrill quarrellings, the squalling of their children, the grunting of their pigs; he smelt the odours of the heaps of garbage in their courtyards: and he was greatly disgusted.

This has the energy of Dickens, only it is Dickens that has gone rancid.

The critics were again positive, though there were one or two dissenting remarks. H.G. Wells complains in an anonymous review: 'Mr Conrad is wordy; his story is not so much told as seen intermittently through a haze of sentences.' Not for the first time (or the last) in his writing career, Conrad is accused of having a prose style that obtrudes on the telling of his tale. Interestingly, when Conrad discovered the name of the reviewer, he wrote to him in considerable excitement. Privately he defended himself:

> My style may be atrocious – but it produces its effect – is as unalterable as say – the size of my feet – and I will never disguise it in boots of Wells's (or anybody else's) making. It would be utter folly. I shall make my own boots or perish.

For a relatively unpractised author, Conrad's self-confidence is surprising. He became friends, of a sort, with Wells though they remained critical of each other. Wells was irritated by Conrad's priest-like devotion to art, and Conrad was unimpressed by Wells' buoyant belief in the value of progress.

Immediately after his marriage to Jessie, Conrad decamped to Normandy. Getting used to Conrad must have been difficult enough, but Jessie was now expected to acclimatise herself to a foreign country. Conrad's motives for this brainwave remain obscure. Possibly, like a lot of married men, he wanted to avoid contact with the wife's relatives; possibly he was seeking social isolation in order to continue writing.

They rented a house at Ile Grande near Lannion in Normandy. The domestic side of marriage appealed to him. The woman's place was in the kitchen, but he was prepared to join her there:

> Jessie is immensely amused by the kitchen and spends most of her time trying talk with the girl (who is a perfect treasure). The kitchen is the most splendid and best furnished apartment… so we see it pretty often.

He notes that this is his very first home.

Fortunately, the sexual life of great authors is a closed book, except in the case of Hardy and Richardson, whose sexual fantasies download into their novels in an exuberant fashion. The only thing that might be said of Conrad is that during his honeymoon he wrote the short story 'The Idiots', which tells of a woman who, having given birth to four children who are mentally disabled, stabs her husband with scissors to put an end to his sexual advances. This gruesome motif was to reappear in *The Secret Agent*.

Conrad was finding it difficult to complete any large-scale work. He had abandoned *The Sisters* after fifty pages and *The Rescue*, another Malayan effort, was dwindling into 'rotten twaddle'.

He wrote at this time: 'I have long fits of depression that in a lunatic asylum would be called madness.' Inevitably, he fell ill: first from fever (a recurrence of malaria) and then from gout, a nasty and painful chronic condition which is not as funny as it sounds. In May 1896, he had a shivering fit that lasted a week. Jessie recalled his 'gleaming teeth' and 'shining eyes' as he 'muttered to himself in a strange tongue… to be unable to penetrate the clouded mind or catch one intelligible word was for an young inexperienced girl truly awful.'

To add to the general misery, Conrad learned that he had lost money in a South African gold mining company. Uncle Tadeusz's legacy was whittled down to a few hundred pounds. In September, they returned to England and finally set up house in Stanford-le-Hope, on the Thames Estuary. By all accounts, the semi-detached villa was dingy and cramped; but it was near to their friends, the Hopes.

In spite of the discomfort, Conrad was now working on *The Nigger of the Narcissus*, a short novel that was to be regarded as his first masterpiece. Unusually for Conrad, he was confident both of his ability and of his artistic goal. On 10th January 1897, he wrote to Garnett:

Nigger died on 7th at 6pm; the ship is not home yet. Expected to arrive tonight and be paid off tomorrow. At the End! I can't eat – I dream – nightmares – and scare my wife.

Hard though it is to credit, the word 'nigger' was colloquial in England at this time, but not thought to be derogatory. The American edition, by contrast, was entitled *The Children of the Sea*.

The story explores the solidarity of merchant seamen on the *Narcissus*, and how their solidarity is threatened by Wait, a malingerer who is suffering from terminal tuberculosis, and Donkin, an idle buffoon, who is both manipulative and malign. It is Conrad's first explicitly political novel, and he dissects the shifting power relationships on the ship; but he also exposes the relationship between man and the natural world:

Forward, the lookout man, erect between the flukes of the two anchors, hummed an endless tune, keeping his eyes fixed dutifully ahead in a vacant stare. A multitude of stars coming out in the clear night peopled the emptiness of the sky. They glittered, as if alive above the sea; they surrounded the running ship on all sides; more intense than the eyes of a staring crowd, and as inscrutable as the souls of men.

Contemporary critics assumed the book to be more or less autobiographical. In fact the book is highly literary, and the debt to Maupassant is self-evident: the details of James Wait's demise – the smoothing of the blanket, the two threads of blood, the terrifying vision of death – are to be found in Forrester's death in Maupassant's novel of decadent Parisian society, *Bel-Ami*. When Forrester dies his eyes close 'like two lamps which are extinguished'. When Wait dies his eyes close 'like two lamps overturned together by a sweeping blow'. It is Conrad, of course, who uses the more arresting simile.

Conrad seems to have been quite unconscious of these borrowings; in June 1898, he sent Garnett a copy of the *Nigger* along with *Bel-Ami*. What can be deduced is that the book is rooted in both 'literature' and 'life'. Conrad's experiences in the study were as powerful as his experiences at sea.

The Nigger of the Narcissus was prefaced by one of his most famous pieces of literary criticism, in which he signals his intentions as a writer, artist and moralist. Though indebted to Maupassant's introduction to *Pierre and Jean*, it has its own, unique, slant: 'Art', he claims, 'is a single-minded attempt to render the highest kind of justice to the visible universe, by bringing to light the truth, manifold and one, underlying its every aspect.' Therefore the writer's task 'is by the power of the written word to make you hear, to make you feel; it is, before all, to make you see'. So far, so *fin de siècle*. But then Conrad the ship's captain and Conrad the novelist are weirdly united – for if the artist succeeds he 'shall awaken in the hearts of the beholders that feeling of unavoidable solidarity; of the solidarity of mysterious origin, in toil, in joy, in hope, in uncertain fate, which binds men to each other and all mankind to the visible world'.

In March 1897 the Conrads moved to Ivy Walls, an Elizabethan farmhouse. Jessie showed genuine insight when she wrote:

> It was some time before it dawned on me that he must be feeling the isolation from men of his own standard of intellect. The only man near at hand was dear Mr Hope…

Gradually, Conrad extended his social circle. In August 1897 Conrad made a friend for life in Robert Bontine Cunninghame Graham, who claimed to be descended from Robert II of Scotland. All his life, Conrad was drawn to dashing characters. Cunninghame Graham, five years older than Conrad, had prospected for gold in Spain, and ridden with gauchos. He had also been a professional politician (a Liberal MP), although at the time of his first meeting Conrad, Graham had decided that 'Parliament is a ship of fools…'

Politically speaking, the two men could not possibly find neutral territory. Cunninghame Graham was a socialist: that is, someone who believed in the possible betterment of mankind. Conrad delighted in pouring scorn and contempt on this roseate view, with an energy and focus he dedicates to few of his other correspondents.

> You with your ideals of sincerity, courage and truth are strangely out of place in the epoch of material preoccupations…You are a most hopeless idealist – your aspirations are irrealisable.

To some extent (in a drawling aristocratic fashion) Cunninghame Graham became a revolutionary in thought, if not in deed. Conrad was inspired to express his most pessimistic reflections when facing the idea that political thought might provide a secure foothold for moral action:

> Faith is a myth and beliefs shift like mists on the shore; thoughts vanish; words, once pronounced, die…

> In this world, as I have known it – we are made to suffer without the shadow of a reason, of a cause or of guilt…

> There is no morality, no knowledge and no hope…

> A moment, a twinkling of an eye and nothing remains – but a clot of mud, of cold mud, of dead mud cast into black space, rolling around an extinguished sun.

Hard, presumably, for Graham to think of a suitable response. Conrad is laying it on thick here, partially to provoke his friend, but also to experiment with his own ideas. If he truly believed in this stuff, he would hardly bother to publish another book, let alone become excited (as he does) when one of his stories won him the princely sum of 50 guineas. By articulating his blackest thoughts, he is able to bypass them.

Soon after the move to Ivy Walls, in August 1897, he finished 'The Return', a short story in the manner of Henry James. In this a wife tries to leave her husband, and fails. The problem between the two is the absence of any 'connection'. Even when each, separately, has a moment of revelation, the two of them remain locked in their mutual incomprehension:

> She seemed touched by the emotion of his voice. Her lips quivered a little and she made one faltering step towards him, putting out her hands in a beseeching gesture, when she perceived, just in time, that being absorbed by the tragedy of his life he had absolutely forgotten her very existence.

Garnett gave the story the thumbs down, and Conrad came to regard it as a left-handed production. This is a shame. The writing has a tautness that is not always pervasive in later works such as *Chance* and *Victory* where he returns to romantic and sexual incompatibility. The understatement of 'The Return' was insufficiently prized.

In October 1897 Conrad made another close friend, the twenty-six year old American novelist Stephen Crane. Crane's *The Red Badge of Courage* had been published two years earlier. The novel's effortless clarity and impersonal (bordering on ironic) narration must have appealed to Conrad, who always confessed to struggling with his English prose. Crane's tuberculosis was advanced when Conrad met him, and he only had two years to live.

It is clear that Conrad had an affection for Crane that cut deep. Edward Garnett recalled visiting Crane when Conrad had popped in for tea:

I saw him with Stephen Crane and he was delightfully sunny and bantered 'poor Steve' in the gentlest, most affectionate style, while the latter sat silent… now and then jumping up suddenly and confiding some new project with intensely electric feeling… And Conrad's skeptical answers were couched in the tenderest, most reluctant tone. I can still hear the shades of Crane's poignant friendliness in his cry 'Joseph!' And Conrad's delight in Crane's personality glowed in the shining warmth of his brown eyes.

What appealed to Conrad was Crane's enthusiasm and innocence; yet neither quality was touched by naivety or callousness. As comes across in his writing, Crane can look at the world with fresh-faced directness. For Conrad, master of aloof obliquity, this quality must have struck with considerable force.

Crane had also had 'adventures', often the key, if Conrad was to be impressed: as a journalist he had reported from Florida on a Cuban insurrection against the Spanish, and had dashed off to witness for the *New York Journal* yet another war between the Greeks and the Turks.

Conrad appreciated Crane's writing, but had reservations. For although Crane thought it 'concise' and 'connected', Conrad complained that it was 'never very deep'. 'While one reads of course he is not to be questioned. He is the master of his reader to the very last line – then – apparently for no reason at all – he seems to let go his hold.' He remarked enigmatically to Cunninghame Graham: 'The man does the outside of many things and the inside of some.'

Conrad continued to plod through *The Rescue*, but grew increasingly weary. He desperately wanted to be a well-loved author who made pots of money; but on this issue, the critics were perceptive: 'Mr Conrad is a writer of genius; but his choice of themes, and the uncompromising nature of his methods debar him from attaining popularity.'

He did not grasp that the average reader wants an ending with confetti littering the final pages as the happy couple kiss and make up. As a result much classic English fiction was to remain for him, metaphorically and almost literally, a closed book. Wells claimed that he would pace up and down, muttering 'What is all this about Jane Austen? What is there in her? What is it all about?…'

As Conrad struggled with *The Rescue* his letters became increasingly despondent:

Life passes and it would pass like a dream were it not that the nerves are stretched like fiddle strings. Something always turns up to give a turn to the screw.

The 'something' in this case was Jessie's pregnancy. The baby (Borys) was born on 14th January 1898. Conrad was not present at the birth; indeed, we know exactly what he was up to – he was writing a letter: 'Faith is a myth and beliefs shift like mists on the shore: thoughts vanish; words once pronounced die… only the string of platitudes seems to have no end.' He breaks off from this litany to add a sulky PS:

This letter ruins this morning's post because an infant of male persuasion arrived and made such a row that I could not hear the postman's whistle. It's a fine commentary upon this letter. But salvation lies on being illogical. Still I feel remorse.

Almost immediately Conrad was afflicted with gout. Like many husbands, Conrad abhorred a change to his routine. Despite the fact that Jessie did the work, he liked to run his home in a crisp sailor-like fashion. Richard Curle, who became a close friend, noted:

He never really lost the sea captain's attitude of thinking that orders were to be obeyed and that the work of a house ought to function as smoothly as that of a ship at sea!

Conrad enjoyed bandying about nautical terminology in the cosiest of domestic situations, no doubt to the amusement and irritation of family and friends. John Conrad, the younger son, remembered that 'my father did not like his plate to be over-loaded' and 'looking like the deck cargo of a tramp steamer'. To enjoy food one must have 'a little bit of storage space left' and not be 'loaded to the gunnels'. After Jessie had injured herself, he dubbed her crutches 'outriggers'.

The arrival of Borys did little to lighten Conrad's mood. On a train journey to visit the Cranes, Conrad agreed to travel with Jessie and the baby in the same compartment but, as Jessie notes, 'on no account were we to give any indication that he belonged to our little party.' Alas, the best laid plans. Jessie's sister forgot the autocratic injunction and asked him to pass her the baby's bottle from the rack above his head. 'The whole carriage was convulsed with suppressed merriment.'

Eventually, Conrad worked himself out of his creative impasse with the creation of his fictional alter ego Marlow. He is first put to good use in 'Youth', the glamorised reworking of Conrad's voyage on the *Palestine* (re-named the *Judea*). The story appears to have been completed in May 1898.

Through Marlow, Conrad is able to narrate events and reflect upon them, closely interweaving action and reaction so that they become impossible to separate. Unsurprisingly, 'Youth' rhapsodises youth and its loss: 'Oh the glamour of youth! Oh the fire of it, more dazzling than the flames of the burning ship, throwing a magic light on the wide earth, leaping audaciously to the sky, presently to be quenched by time, more dull, more pitiless, and more bitter than the sea – and like the flames of the burning ship surrounded by impenetrable night.'

'Youth' is possibly Conrad's most optimistic work, even if it does remind us that to be young is to be coupled 'with the strength, with the romance of illusions.' In his next two stories, Marlow's role becomes both more complex and more ambiguous.

Whilst staying with Edward Garnett in September 1898 Conrad met the writer who was to have the greatest impact on his work, if not his life, Ford Madox Ford. Ford was twenty-four and already publishing. As the grandson of the Pre-Raphaelite painter and the son of the music critic of *The Times*, Ford was at the heart of the Victorian artistic establishment and had a knack for networking. He was married to Elsie Martindale, described by David Garnett as 'high breasted and dark' with 'a rich, high colour, like a ripe nectarine'.

Ford took to Conrad at once and offered to sublet his rented house, Pent Farm in Postling, Kent. The Conrads accepted the kind offer and moved in on 26th October. Although the house appeared initially to lack water, gas and electricity, it was pretty, and Conrad appreciated the views:

> The colouring of the country presents brown and pale yellow tints – and in between, in the distance, one can see the meadows as green as emeralds.

Given that much of his childhood was spent exiled in Russian wastelands, the absence of a few amenities would not prove insurmountable. As ever, Jessie would have to make the best of it. Conrad's biographers tend to give Ford rather a drubbing. He is seen as a potentially talented opportunist who hitched a ride on genius to further his career. It is worth bearing in mind that Ford was himself a writer of the first rank, whose *Good Soldier* and *Parade's End* are worthy to stand alongside Conrad at his best; and although Ford's memoirs stretch the truth, it is worth recalling that Conrad himself was not averse to tinkering with the facts if they proved inconvenient.

Without doubt, Ford was always fond of Conrad. He recalls their first meeting:

> He had the gestures of a Frenchman who shrugs his shoulders frequently. When you had really secured his attention

he would insert a monocle into his right eye and scrutinise your face from near as a watchmaker looks into the works of a watch… He spoke English with great fluency and distinction, with correctitude in his syntax, his words absolutely exact as to meaning but his accentuation so faulty that he was at times difficult to understand and his use of adverbs as often as not eccentric… He gesticulated with his hands and shoulders when he wished to be emphatic, but when he forgot himself in the excitement of talking he gesticulated with his whole body…

Evidently Conrad never lost his 'heavy foreign' accent, an accent which set him apart, and yet was not easy to place. Once he was asked (by Richard Curle's son) what he thought of the view from his own house. 'Too many orcs!' he snapped. The company fell silent, until pennies dropped. Oaks.

One of the most difficult questions to resolve is to discover who the leading light was behind the Ford–Conrad collaboration. Eventually they were to write three novels together, *The Inheritors* (1901), *Romance* (1903), and *The Nature of a Crime* (1924). One of the advantages of Pent Farm was that Conrad found himself amongst a nest of famous writers, most of whom he admired: apart from Wells (Sandgate) there was Kipling (Rottingdean) and grandest of all literary grandees, Henry James, who had taken up residence in Rye. None of this bunch could imagine that Conrad had suggested the idea of writing with Ford, and assumed Ford was the villain of the peace, chancing his arm as usual. Indeed James threw up his hands in camp horror, a behavioural mode he found especially congenial in his final phase:

To me this is like a bad dream which one relates at breakfast! Their traditions and their gifts are so dissimilar. Collaboration between them is to me inconceivable.

The truth is that the idea originated with Conrad, who was, as ever, hard-up. Writing to W.E. Henley, editor of the *New Review*, he admits:

> When talking with Ford my first thought was that the man there who couldn't find a publisher had some good stuff to use and that if we worked it up together my name, probably, would get a publisher for it. On the other hand I thought that working with him would keep under the particular devil that spoils my work for me as quick as I turn it out… and that the material being of the kind that appeals to my imagination and the man being an honest workman we could turn out something tolerable – perhaps.

Whatever the exact truth, Conrad believed himself in charge. The simple fact is that he wanted a bestseller and Ford seemed to provide him with a means to that particular end. Besides, collaborations had been successfully accomplished by both Dumas and Stevenson. It is also possible that Ford could help Conrad master a more colloquial and flexible English. Violet Hunt, who became Ford's mistress, was in no doubt who led the partnership:

> Ford adored Conrad. I never heard him speak of Conrad without the most reverent affection… In matters of literature his attitude was servile, positively.

Just as Ford revered Conrad, so Conrad revered James, both as a writer and as a man. His first overture was to send James an elaborately inscribed copy of *An Outcast of the Islands*. In February 1897, James replied with an equally flattering message in the flyleaf of *The Spoils of Poynton*. When they eventually met, they were so courteous, it was difficult to grasp what they were saying. And for reasons that remained forever impenetrable to those who witnessed these literary panjandrums in action, they spoke to each other in French: Conrad honking *'Mon cher maître'*, in a thick Marseille accent, whilst James replied *'Mon cher confrère'* with lofty condescension.

Possibly, James found Conrad's nervous, excitable manner put him more on edge than usual; possibly he felt that Conrad expected of him more than he was prepared, or able, to offer. Whatever the reasons, the relationship withered, rather than flourished. In an essay on James in 1905, Conrad describes him as 'the historian of fine consciences'. He goes on to praise James, but also to illuminate potential limitations:

> he has mastered the country, this domain, not wild indeed, but full of romantic glimpses, of deep shadows and sunny places. There are no secrets left within his range. He has disclosed them as they should be disclosed – that is, beauti-fully. And indeed ugliness has but little place in this world of his creation.

It is clear from all that Conrad wrote, that he believed the absence of ugliness can only be regarded as a wilful distortion of truth.

On 3rd June 1898, Conrad refers in a letter for the first time to *Lord Jim*. The genesis of this novel was protracted and painful, even by Conrad's standards. In February 1899, he assures his new publisher Blackwood that he is veering towards completion of the story, which he still assumes will be brief – between twenty and thirty thousand words. But in the previous December he had started work on *Heart of Darkness*. It would appear that *Lord Jim* and *Heart of Darkness* were written in tandem, and that Conrad was exploring similar ideas in both works, simultaneously. *Heart of Darkness* reached the finishing post first. He completed 38,000 words on 6th February 1899. It was serialised in *Blackwood's* magazine prefaced by the definite article.

Heart of Darkness remains Conrad's most celebrated chef d'oeuvre, not least because of Coppola's fanciful film adaptation,

Apocalypse Now. It is a tale with something for everybody: exotic travel, racism, metaphysics and politics are all presented with shifting ambiguity.

The story has an unnamed narrator who (with others) listens to Marlow spin his yarn whilst they wait on the Thames for a favourable tide. He warns us early on that for Marlow 'the meaning of an episode was not inside like a kernel but outside enveloping the tale which brought it out only as a glow brings out a haze...'

Marlow opens by contemplating the colonial experience of the Romans in Britain, though he does not like to call them colonists:

> They were conquerors, and for that you want only brute force – nothing to boast of, when you have it, since your strength is just an accident arising from the weakness of others... The conquest of the earth, which mostly means the taking it away from those who have a different complexion or slightly flatter noses than ourselves, is not a pretty thing when you look into it too much.

These observations control our reading of Marlow's experiences.

Marlow finds himself in Belgium, out of work; he gets a job in the Congo, with the help of an aunt. The white man is shown as inefficient, cruel, lazy and self-indulgent. The Congolese are portrayed as pitiful slaves: 'I could see every rib, the joints of their limbs were like knots in a rope; each had an iron collar on his neck and all connected together.' Marlow's problem (which he never spelt out) is that as an employee of the company, he is partially responsible for all he sees. Far from being a disinterested observer, he is helping to promote Belgian imperialism. To keep this thought at bay, he becomes involved with Mr Kurtz. Kurtz is a 'first class' agent who is in charge of a trading post which gathers more ivory than anyone else. He is also a liberal intellectual who goes to the Congo in the name of civilisation and progress.

The story then takes the form of a quest up river, not for the lost treasure of King Solomon, or an enormous gorilla, but for an intelligent kind-hearted reformer who, it turns out, has turned into a monster. When Marlow finds Kurtz in the heart of the interior, it is clear that he has been indulging in 'unspeakable rites'. Shrunken heads surrounded his hut. The wilderness 'had caressed him... it had taken him, loved him and embraced him, got into his veins, consumed his flesh and sealed his soul!'

Here, Kurtz's Faustian pact with the wilderness is made explicit. What he actually did has to be inferred: it seems he was worshipped as a god, lived with a native girlfriend and is likely to have been involved with cannibalism. On the voyage down river, Kurtz dies, uttering the immortal words 'out twice, a cry that was no more than a breath – The horror! The horror!' The significance of this perception is left hanging. When Marlow finally returns to England, half-dead with illness, he visits Kurtz's intended (his fiancée) and re-writes Kurtz's death in terms of sentimental Victorian fiction. Marlow, who prides himself on his truth-telling, looks her squarely in the eye and tells her 'The last word he pronounced was – your name!'

As Marlow lies to support Kurtz, he seals his pact with him, just as surely as Kurtz had sealed his own pact with the wilderness. When Marlow stops talking, the narrator realises that they have missed the tide: Marlow's story has paralysed them. This is a nicely ironic touch, because Marlow constantly reiterates the responsibilities of work, and yet has here prevented others from pursuing their duty.

Because *Heart of Darkness* exposes the shallowness of good intentions when confronted by primitive drives, it seemed prescient of the barbarities that afflicted mid-twentieth century Europe. Its exposure of the mercenary motives that lurk behind colonial expansion also went down a storm as the old European empires crumbled into compromise and withdrawal. Conrad himself exempted the British from these strictures and remained a British patriot: having suffered under Russian autocracy, he appreciated democratic freedom sufficiently to turn a blind eye to his adopted countrymen though he had doubts about British conduct in the Boer War:

> If I am to believe Kipling this is a war undertaken for the cause of democracy. C'est à crever de rire.

On the other hand he is swift to clarify the issue by suggesting that 'This was not so much a war against the Transvaal as a struggle against the doings of German influence. It is the Germans who have forced the issue...'

The need to defend his adopted homeland ties Conrad in knots. In a letter to his Polish cousin, he admits:

> Much might be said about the war. My feelings are very complex – as you may guess. That they – the Boers – are struggling in good faith for their independence cannot be doubted; but it is also a fact that they have no idea of liberty, which can only be found under the English flag all over the world.

The dislike of the Dutch harks back to his days out East. Without doubt, the South African war depressed him, as did the sloth-like progress on *Lord Jim*. He wrote to Ted Sanderson in terms of aching despondency:

> I am now trying to finish a story which began in the Oct. No. of Blackwood. I am at it day after day, and I want all day every minute of a day, to produce a beggarly tale of words or perhaps to produce nothing at all... And when that is finished... I must go on even go on at once and drag out of myself another 20,000 words if the boy is to have his milk and I my beer (this is a figure of speech – I don't drink beer,

I drink weak tea and yearn after dry champagne) and if the world is not absolutely to come to an end.

Conrad turns writing into a painful duty: he does not see writing as a playful flight of the imagination, but as a sober task to be completed with care. It is as if he were back on the rolling deck of a clapped out merchant ship with only bad weather ahead of him.

The household at Pent Farm centred on Conrad who was not to be disturbed when writing. This would be reasonable, except that he worked at erratic hours, whenever gripped by inspiration. Not for him the stately organisation of an Anthony Trollope. Jessie recalls one occasion when he

> stalked through the dining room with the terse request that I should at once prepare him a dose of gout medicine. He then announced to all and sundry his intention of retiring to the next room and trying to rest. He wished to be alone there... Totally disregarding his guests who looked... uncomfortable, he closed one door after another behind him with considerable violence... Later he reappeared refreshed after his nap, and quite ready to make himself agreeable, both his irritation and threatened gout gone!

Time and again, Conrad displays a disconcerting mixture of self-absorption and self-dramatisation. Were he a toddler, he would be accused of attention-seeking. And like a child, he had the habit of making bread pellets and flinging them about the room. Jessie recalls that 'the more excited or irritated he got, the quicker flew the missiles and those in the line of fire would look appreciatively at their host.' Hard to believe that this is the same Conrad who could be so preternaturally courteous to Henry James.

Lord Jim was finished early in the morning of 14th July 1900. It ran to over 140,000 words: Conrad's initial estimation had been in the region of 20,000. Writing to Galsworthy, Conrad describes the last agonising moments of its birth:

> The end of *L. J.* has been pulled off with a steady drag of 21 hours. I sent wife and child out of the house (to London) and sat down at 9 am with a desperate resolve to be done with it. Now and then I took a walk round the house out of one door in the other. Ten-minute meals. A great hush. Cigarette ends growing into a mound similar to a cairn over a dead hero. Moon rose over the barn looked in at the window and climbed out of sight. Dawn broke, brightened. I put the lamp out and went on, with the morning breeze blowing the sheets of MS all over the room. Sun rose. I wrote the last word and went into the dining room. Six o'clock. I shared a piece of cold chicken with Escamillo...

Conrad's celebration with the dog is comfortingly cheerless.

Lord Jim was Conrad's most complex and profound work to date. Jim is not an intellectual like Kurtz, but he suffers similarly from self-betrayal: absence of self-knowledge leads both into acts of supreme cowardice. Kurtz abandons his ideals, Jim his professional duty.

The novel opens with a blast of derisive irony as Conrad anatomises the complacencies of Jim's upbringing.

> Originally he came from a parsonage. Many commanders of fine merchant-ships come from these abodes of piety and peace. Jim's father possessed such certain knowledge of the Unknowable as made for the righteousness of people in cottages without disturbing the ease of mind of those whom unerring Providence enables to live in mansions... Jim was one of five sons, and when after a course of light holiday literature his vocation for the sea had declared itself, he was sent at once to a 'training-ship for officers of the mercantile marine.'

(Does Conrad suspect that he himself chose the Merchant Service only because he had Fenimore Cooper and Marryat swilling about in his head?)

From the start we are aware that Jim has committed a crime. As the perspective shifts to Marlow and his story of the court case we learn that Jim and the rest of the crew had abandoned a bunch of pilgrims on an overcrowded rust bucket that they reckoned would sink. Faced with a sudden emergency, Jim's nerve fails him, as it did once before, when he was an apprentice. He tells Marlow how he came to abandon ship: "'I had jumped...'" He checked himself, averted his gaze... "It seems," he added.'

The guilt compounded with the evasion of responsibility is as disturbing as Marlow's realisation that Jim is 'one of us'. Only by being tested do we know ourselves, but fortunately most of us are never called to offer proof of courage. Marlow finds Jim's story nibbles away at his own moral certainties.

The novel tells the story of Jim's attempts to atone and find redemption. Because Conrad's world is devoid of religious consolation, this proves a struggle. With the help of Stein, philosopher and entomologist, Jim is sent to an isolated trading post in Patusan, a remote Malay district of a native ruled state.

Stein's analysis of Jim could be Conrad's analysis of his younger Marseille self: 'his thoughts would be full of valorous deeds: he loved these dreams and the success of his imaginary achievements... They had a gorgeous virility, the charm of vagueness, they passed before him with a heroic tread... There was nothing he could not face.'

In some respects *Lord Jim* is as close as Conrad came to writing a *Portrait of the Artist as a Young Man*: but Conrad's self portrayal is far more devastating than Joyce's affectionately teasing glimpses of Stephen Dedalus/Joyce. *Lord Jim* is less concerned with betrayal, than the protagonist's appalling lack of self-understanding. In the closing pages of the novel, when he dies, as a sort of benevolent Kurtz, defending the natives from the pasteboard villain Gentleman Brown, Jim fails to grasp that his carefully manufactured self-sacrifice does not prove anything: if the test of a man's character is the unexpected, then Jim's carefully staged tragic exit does nothing to wipe away his desertion of the pilgrims. 'He passes away under a cloud, inscrutable at heart, forgotten, unforgiven and excessively romantic.'

Conrad's 'desertion' of Poland is sometimes seen to be the clue in his fascination with Jim's predicament, because he wrote of his departure as a 'jump': 'I verily believe mine was the only case of a boy of my nationality and antecedents taking a, so to speak, standing jump out of his radical surrounding and association.' Conrad's self-analysis is more profound: he sees himself as pathologically attached to ideals that are unattainable and that he is always doomed to spoil: ideals of conduct, of work, of literary ambition. *Lord Jim* gives a clue to Conrad's relentless sense of failure, as soon as he puts pen to paper.

The last instalment of *Lord Jim* appeared on 25th October 1900. The book was initially acclaimed as the author's 'greatest work', 'entirely original', bringing Conrad 'into the front rank of living novelists'. But there were caveats: critics felt uneasy with the involved methods of narration and Arnold Bennett moaned that *Lord Jim* was 'more than a little difficult to read'. The first impression was sold out in two months, but the next lasted four years: Conrad's reputation had increased, but his bank balance showed few signs of recovery. Within months Conrad was borrowing from insurance companies, his publisher Blackwood, anyone who was prepared to cough up.

Conrad was now coupled with Kipling as a writer of exotic romances. This irritated Conrad who admired Kipling's talent, but disliked his conservative triumphalism. In a letter to Cunninghame Graham, he mixes mild contempt with characteristic hauteur:

Mr Kipling has the wisdom of the passing generations – and holds it in perfect sincerity. Some of his work is of impeccable form and because of that little thing he shall sojourn in Hell only a very short while. He squints with the rest of his excellent sort.

With *Lord Jim* finished, Conrad decided to take the family on holiday with Ford in tow, whilst they worked on 'Seraphina' together. Conrad's family holidays were usually cursed. Bruges and Ostend are not often dangerous destinations: remarkably enough just outside Ostend, Borys nearly died, after contracting dysentery. Even Jessie had to admit that Ford behaved himself:

> he earned my gratitude and appreciation by the manner he showed his practical sympathy. He was always at hand to shift any small invalid, fetch the doctor or help with the nursing.

As he was to reveal later in his dealings with the glitterati of the modernist movement, Ford was essentially a kind man.

On their return to Kent, the literary collaboration continued, to the consternation of Jessie, who found having two authors in a smallish cottage troublesome. Conrad's foibles were more than enough, as Jessie notes with her usual tone of controlled exasperation:

> The small house seemed at times full to overflowing and there were days when the two artists with their vagaries, temperaments and heated discussions made it seem rather a warm place. Still to give Ford his due, he was the least peppery of the two, being a native of a less excitable nation and his drawling voice made a sharp contrast with the quick un-English utterances of the fellow collaborator.

It looks as if Ford and Conrad discussed what they were to write, then went away and pushed pens separately. There is never any suggestion of Ford stooping over Conrad correcting his grammar, or Conrad egging Ford on to varnish his prose with a glamorous sheen.

Frankly, both *The Inheritors* and 'Seraphina' are duds, and not particularly interesting duds, at that. *The Inheritors* tells the tale of Etchingham Granger, an English gentleman, who meets a young woman who is a Fourth Dimensionist. Fourth Dimensionists are a people with super powers (but no emotion), who will eventually inherit the earth. She succeeds in wrecking a scheme to exploit Greenland and the Dimensionists triumph. The bolting on of fantasy to satire had been done before, but Swift's talents were of a different order, and neither Conrad nor Ford have the required lightness of touch: the satiric targets are haphazard, the writing elegantly stupid. The narrator blathers:

> The girl was a riddle and a riddle once guessed is a very trivial thing. She, too, would be a very trivial thing when I had found a solution. It occurred to me that she wished me to regard her as a symbol, perhaps, of the future…

The prose is self-generating: once cranked into action, there seems no reason why it should ever grind to a halt.

Romance (as 'Seraphina' was eventually titled) is minor Stevenson with water; Rider Haggard without the unconscious psychological peculiarities. It tells of the aristocratic hero John Kemp and his adventures. He narrates his story in a fashion that mixes breathless urgency with static *longueur*:

> All this is in my mind now, softened by distance, by the tenderness of things remembered – the wonderful dawn of life, with all the mystery and promise of the young day breaking amongst heavy thunder-clouds. At the time I was overwhelmed – I can't express it otherwise. I felt like a man thrown out to sink or swim, trying to keep his head above water.

Whether Ford or Conrad was responsible for this soup of portentous platitude, it is fortunately impossible to guess. Conrad hoped that the novel might bring popular success and, more importantly, give him a financial boost. It did neither. The critics were sniffy and, luckily for Conrad, were inclined to blame Ford for the novel's self-evident shortcomings.

The Master
1903–11

After the disappointment of *Romance*, Conrad returned to tinkering with *The Rescue*, the Malayan novel that was still floating in the doldrums. Almost casually he wrote to Galsworthy at this time to tell him that he was 'full of a story' but that 'I have not been able to write a single word – except the title, which shall be, I think: *Nostromo*.'

Nostromo was to bring Conrad to the verge of mental breakdown. It was also to prove to be undisputedly one of his finest achievements, a novel conceived on a vast scale, written with consistent intensity. By August 1903, he had written 42,000 words. He tells Pinker (his publisher / friend / Tadeusz substitute): 'It is very genuine Conrad. At the same time it is more of a Novel pure and simple than anything I've done since *Almayer's Folly...*' He goes on to lament: 'I daren't draw a cheque.' The combination of ferocious concentration on work and financial worry was bearing down on Conrad pitilessly.

Biographers and critics seem to evade the difficult question of why he tackled this immense panoramic novel at this stage of his career. In my own view, after labouring on *Lord Jim* and *Heart of Darkness*, both, in some sense, semi-autobiographical attempts to come to terms with elements of his personality and of his past, Conrad felt free to write a 'Novel, pure and simple'. In other words, for almost the first time, Conrad is not dredging up material from his youth, but contemplating the world 'from the outside'. As a result, *Nostromo* is almost deliriously imaginative, showing few signs of the weariness which pervades Conrad's letters at this time, and of all his novels, it is the one most rooted in reading and research. Conrad had to supplement his 'glimpse' of South America with histories of Paraguay and Venezuela.

Nostromo is a story of South American revolution, American capitalist colonialism, and the crumbling of political dreams. It is populated with an astonishing cast of characters who are treated, almost universally, with acidulous irony, as their selflessness is exposed as self interest. Charles Gould, who initially becomes involved with his father's silver mine in Conrad's fictional province of Sulaco to preserve his father's memory, becomes a slave to 'material interests':

> it hurt Charles Gould to feel that never more, by no effort of will, would he be able to think of his father in the same way he used to think of him when the poor man was alive. His breathing image was no longer in his power. This consideration, closely affecting his own identity, filled his breast with a mournful and angry desire for action. In this his instinct was unerring. Action is consolatory. It is the enemy of thought and the friend of flattering illusions. Only in the conduct of our action can we find the sense of mastery over the Fates.

Action no longer has the redeeming possibility that it contained in *Heart of Darkness*.

The novel takes place in Conrad's fictional state of Costaguana (literally shit coast, or, more politely, coast of droppings). Hovering over the revolutionaries is the enigmatic American millionaire Mr Holroyd, who exploits inherent political instability for his own ends, whilst camouflaging his actions in a veil of Christian and humanitarian concern. Conrad's prescience in sensing the dangers of aggressive American capitalism, and its relationship to 'indirect' colonialism, is remarkable. 'Time itself has got to wait on the greatest country in the whole of God's universe' says the American millionaire and 'endower of churches':

> we shall be giving the word for everything: industry, trade, law, journalism, art, politics, and religion, from Cape Horn clear over to Smith's Sound and beyond, too, if anything worth taking hold of turns up at the North Pole... We shall run the world's business whether the world like it or not. The world can't help it – and neither can we, I guess.

Nostromo is traditionally viewed as a 'difficult' novel because of its relentless scepticism and its multi-layered narrative. The story moves back and forth in time to expose the fallacy of 'progress'. Politics is viewed as disguised greed. Caught in the heart of this maelstrom are Martin Decoud, a disaffected journalist who joins the political cause to impress the woman he loves, and Nostromo, the leader of the dock workers. (Nostromo is a contraction of 'Our Man', the patronising title awarded him by his employers.)

Both find themselves on a mission to smuggle silver out of the Sulaco Gulf. In the darkness, their boat is damaged and they are compelled to conceal the treasure on a nearby island. Decoud is left to guard the silver, but the isolation of the island erodes his sense of self. Unable to bear the loneliness Decoud shoots himself: 'He died from solitude, the enemy known but to few on this earth and whom only the simplest of us are fit to withstand.' As for Nostromo, he begins to pilfer the hidden treasure, in secret as he realises that his sense of duty has been exploited by those around him. He becomes quietly rich, but coated in self-loathing: 'his courage, his magnificence, his leisure, his work, everything was as before, only everything is a sham.'

Mrs Gould, the wife of the owner of the San Tome (and one of Conrad's most convincing female characters) reflects ruefully towards the end of the novel on the power of 'material interests' and how it corrodes political and moral idealism:

she saw the San Tome mountain hanging over the Campo, over the whole land feared, hated, wealthy; more soulless than any tyrant, more pitiless and autocratic than the worst Government; ready to crush innumerable lives in the expansion of its greatness.

It is impossible to do justice to the scope and intelligence of *Nostromo*. Few twentieth century novels come within hailing distance.

In personal terms, it cost Conrad dearly. Despite the jocular remark in his 'Author's Note' that, on finishing the book, he found the 'family all well, my wife heartily glad to learn that the fuss was all over, and our small boy considerably grown during my absence', the truth was more dramatic. Throughout the writing of the novel, he was both physically ill and psychologically not at his best. On meeting the writer and poet Sir Henry Newbolt at the Savile Club, Newbolt asked him why he was leaving London. Conrad replied that the streets terrified him:

'terrified – by that dull stream of obliterated faces.' He leaned forward with both hands raised and clenched. 'Yes, terrified: I see their personalities all leaping out at me like tigers!'

There is no particular reason to believe that Conrad was teasing.

Predictably enough, *Nostromo* was not a popular success, and the critics were guarded. The *Times Literary Supplement* complained that 'the drama is overwhelmed by the machinery', going on to declare roundly that its publication 'as it stands is an artistic mistake'. Even if the reviewers attempted to be tactful and deferential, their crassness must have stung Conrad, who sensed that he had written a masterpiece. The *British Weekly* recommended the novel as a cracking 'adventure story'. Jessie believed that '*Nostromo*'s reception was perhaps the greatest disappointment – literary disappointment – Conrad ever had.'

Whilst he was working on the novel, Conrad took a flat in Kensington. Financially speaking this was a puzzling move, since Conrad's bank, Watson and Company, had failed, leaving him semi-broke once again. 'Two fifty gone at one swoop.'

If this were not enough, there was also a medical emergency. In January, on a shopping expedition to Barkers (the department store), Jessie tripped on the pavement badly injuring both her knees. Her weight ensured that the physical damage was severe. There were devastating consequences when she found herself an invalid, requiring expensive treatment.

During the writing of *Nostromo* and the light autobiography *The Mirror of the Sea*, Conrad and Jessie traipsed between Kent and London depending on the state of her condition. In November, she was placed in a nursing home and endured a complicated operation. Initially, this appeared successful but it eventually transpired that it made the original damage much worse. Despite the bad news Conrad was in relatively high spirits as he continued to churn out his sea sketches. Indeed, Jessie complained that the evening before her stay in the nursing home, Conrad had thoughtfully invited thirty people to dinner.

It is hard to avoid the conclusion that Conrad was now entering some sort of manic phase. His next move was to plan a four month break on the island of Capri. He hoped this would help Jessie in her recovery and perhaps alleviate his persistent attacks of gout.

The Conrads' holidays were usually calamitous. At Dover, one of the men carrying Jessie on to the ferry pinched his hand on the gangway rail and almost dumped her into the Channel. In Rome, she was left suspended from a railway carriage because her chair was removed too enthusiastically. When they finally managed to land Jessie at Capri – a saga in itself – Conrad caught influenza and topped it off with bronchitis, neither of which helped his insomnia. Still, he overcame these to be fit enough to face a raging toothache which blew up his face like a balloon. Inevitably, there was no dentist in Capri, so he had to visit Naples where two teeth were extracted painfully.

By early May, Conrad was finding the novelty of the climate and scenery somewhat wearing. Nor was he particularly tickled by the gay goings on, despite befriending the future novelist Norman Douglas, whose louche parties were notorious. He wrote to Ford:

> The scandals of Capri – atrocious, unspeakable, amusing, scandals international, cosmopolitan and biblical… All this is a sort of blue nightmare traversed by stinks and perfumes… vineyards… kodaks, floating veils strangely waving whiskers, grotesque hats.

And German tourists, for whom he had a particular contempt: 'It is a nightmare with the fear of the future thrown in.'

Although Conrad attempted to write whilst in Capri, it was almost useless. As he reflects to Edmund Gosse: 'I, in my state of honourable adoption, find that I need the moral support, the sustaining influence of English atmosphere, even from day to day.'

He did manage to pen *Autocracy and War*, a response to the Russo-Japanese War. After praising the gentleness of the Japanese, he laid into the Russians with considerable enthusiasm. The Russian State is portrayed somewhat luridly as a crude despotic tyranny, essentially primitive and un-European: 'something not of this world, partaking of a ravenous ghoul'. Although the essay is schematic, it is clear Conrad's mind is turning towards the issue that would permeate both *The Secret Agent* and *Under Western Eyes*.

Conrad returned home to discover that he had been awarded the princely sum of £500 from the Royal Bounty Fund. Edmund Gosse, who moved in posh and influential circles, had touched on the matter with Balfour, the Prime Minister. The King himself was supposed to have approved the grant.

Inevitably, this boon turned out to be more complicated than expected. Obviously enough, Conrad expected a cheque to be handed over without delay. Unfortunately, his reputation preceded him and it was decided that two trustees would be appointed to look after the money for him, handing it over in dribs and drabs. Conrad was angry; after all, he had debts that needed paying. Henry Newbolt, one of the trustees, was assaulted by dramatic letters that were both argumentative and self-justificatory. The bartering revealed the gap between an Establishment that believed Conrad should behave with bourgeois propriety, and Conrad, who still saw himself as a displaced Polish aristocrat who needed both to face financial difficulties, and also to enjoy a well upholstered standard of living. At heart, he was still a *szlachta*. The episode left him much the worse for wear, though once he was finally released from some of his debts, he cheered up sufficiently to continue work on a variety of projects: though it has to be said that, between 1905 and 1906, there is a lack of focus.

As ever, there were the usual domestic and medical mishaps: Borys caught scarlet fever, Jessie had a 'nervous breakdown of a sort', Conrad himself was afflicted with gout. It says something of the Conrads' affection for each other, or of the unguessable weirdness of all marital relations, that in the middle of this downpour of misfortune, Jessie discovered that she was pregnant. Conrad was fifty, Jessie thirty-four. He told an acquaintance: 'I feel very shy and blushing at being let in for this thing at my venerable age.' To cheer Jessie up, Conrad took her to stay at the (improbably named) Hotel Riche in Montpellier. In these plush surroundings, Conrad set to work on *The Secret Agent*, his novel of anarchists and tinpot revolutionaries who lurk in the grime of London, the 'cruel devourer of the world's light'.

On 2nd August, in a Kensington house borrowed from Galsworthy, Conrad's second son was born. John Alexander's relationship with his father was always less fraught than Borys', whose bouts of illness must have made him something of an anxiety. Possibly, because he was the second son, less was expected of him; possibly Conrad's advanced years had softened his parental approach.

Throughout the summer and autumn of 1906, Conrad continued on *The Secret Agent*, which he finished in November. The 'Author's Note' roots the inspiration for the book in two separate 'incidents'. Talking to a friend (possibly Ford): 'we recalled the already old story of the attempt to blow up the Greenwich Observatory.' The friend 'then remarked in his characteristically casual and omniscient manner: "Oh, that fellow was half an idiot. His sister committed suicide afterwards."'

The other source he mentions was a remark found in an Assistant Commissioner of Police's memoirs:

the author... reproduced a short dialogue held in the Lobby of the House of Commons after some unexpected anarchist outrage, with the Home Secretary. The phrase... that struck me most was Sir W. Harcourt's [the then Home Secretary] angry sally: 'All that's very well. But your idea of secrecy over there seems to consist of keeping the Home Secretary in the dark.'

Conrad continues: 'all of a sudden I felt myself stimulated.'

The story of *The Secret Agent* is grim enough. A lazy and incompetent secret agent is ordered by his Russian superiors to commit an anarchist outrage. Having commissioned a bomb, he decides to use his mentally retarded 'idiot' brother-in-law to blow up Greenwich Observatory. The brother-in-law stumbles and blows himself into little pieces. Nevertheless he is identified by the nametag on his coat. The police call. Winnie Verloc, the secret agent's wife, discovers that her husband has murdered her beloved brother. She, in turn, murders him with a kitchen knife and later commits suicide, flinging herself from a train. Out of this melodramatic material, Conrad fashioned a novel which is both profound and comic.

Before his marriage to Winnie, Verloc stayed at her mother's lodging house intermittently:

> He came and went without any very apparent reason. He generally arrived in London (like the influenza) from the Continent, only he arrived unheralded by the Press; and his visitations set in with great severity. He breakfasted in bed, and remained wallowing there with an air of quiet enjoyment till noon every day – and sometimes even to a later hour.

All the characters, all the incidents of the novel, are described in a tone of aggressive irony that is relentlessly funny, never more so than when least appropriate. Chief Inspector Heat here examines Stevie's remains:

> Another waterproof sheet was spread over that table in the manner of a tablecloth, with the corners turned up over a sort of mound – a heap of rags, scorched and bloodstained, half concealing what might have been an accumulation of raw material for a cannibal feast. It required considerable firmness of mind not to recoil before the sight. Chief Inspector Heat, an efficient officer of his department, stood his ground, but for a whole minute he did not advance. A local constable in uniform cast a sidelong glance, and said with stolid simplicity:
>   'He's all there. Every bit of him. It was a job.'

Conrad marries the domestic tragedy of a man who stolidly refuses to understand his wife, with an analysis of the relationship between anarchist terrorists and society, as represented by the police and the government. One of the most extreme of the anarchists, the Professor, walks the streets of London with a bomb in his pocket, prepared to blow himself up if ever arrested. Outside the law, he infuriates the police because he refuses to play by the rules. Conrad recognised that both regular criminals and those who enforce the law are essentially involved in the same game. The Professor frightens because he has torn up the rulebook. He is seen, in the last paragraph of the novel: 'insignificant, shabby, miserable – and terrible in the simplicity of his idea calling madness and despair to the regeneration of the world. Nobody looked at him. He passed on unsuspected and deadly, like a pest in the street full of men.' The power of this climax is achieved because, for once, Conrad modulates the ironic tone and the baleful levity shifts to something darker.

Because we live in a world of daily terrorist outrages, of casual suicide bombings, of beliefs that are happily wedded to acts of cruelty and violence, *The Secret Agent* is Conrad's most popular novel at the beginning of the twenty-first century. Only a few weeks after 9/11, journalists were quoting Conrad with glee. Once more, he seems a century or so ahead of his time.

As ever, the contemporary critics displayed their usual mixture of respect and obtuseness. The *Manchester Guardian*, for instance, complained that 'his revolutionaries and their opponents are not engaging', whilst *Country Life* found the complicated method of narration all too much. As the reviewers of the *Athenaeum* noted, with genuine perspicacity: 'the keenness of his artistic senses have placed him further away from the great reading public – if infinitely nearer to the select few who have trained faculties of literary appreciation – than many a writer of far less worth.'

Conrad found himself in the dire position of being classed a 'great writer' who nobody much would want to read. No wonder that he grumbled that he was feeling 'horribly seedy and depressed'.

On 16th December the family left once more for Montpellier. Conrad rested. The following month Borys was diagnosed with infected adenoids and a few weeks later he caught measles: after that, bronchitis set in, with suspected tuberculosis.

Given that both Conrad's parents died of the disease, this must have been a particularly worrying time. Fortunately, the diagnosis proved incorrect, and Conrad moved the family on to Geneva, seeking a hydropathic cure for his gout. This was to be paid for by Pinker, his agent, until Conrad finished work on his next novel, *Chance*. (Pinker was constantly bailing Conrad out.) Unfortunately, just before they left for Switzerland both Borys and John contracted whooping cough. Conrad noted that John 'had melted down to half his size. Since yesterday morning he had a coughing fit every quarter of an hour and so will not eat anything... My dear Pinker I feel that all this is almost too much for me.' As Conrad declined, Jessie rose to the challenge. He wrote of her: 'Jessie has been simply heroic in the awful Montpellier adventure, never giving a sign of anxiety not only before the boy but even out of his sight.' Whatever his mood, Conrad remained appreciative of Jessie's efforts and loyally affectionate. John recovered relatively quickly, and Borys remained unwell for five months.

They had returned to Pent in the summer of 1907. Conrad wrote that he was sick of 'trips abroad' and, true to his word, he stayed in England for the next seven years. But he decided to leave Pent; in September, he moved to Someries, in Bedfordshire. This was to be the first of three moves between 1907 and 1910. One way or another, Conrad's restlessness was doomed to find expression, if not intellectually, then physically.

As was his gloominess. Of Someries, he complained to Ellie Hueffer, Ford's wife: 'You have no idea of the soul corroding bleakness of earth and sky here when the east wind blows.' At times, he unconsciously echoes his exiled father's words in Volgada. It is tempting to suggest that Conrad remained forever a wanderer in exile – but oddly, one with the full paraphernalia of an Edwardian family in tow.

Bored with Someries, Conrad visited Ford, who was starting up a new literary magazine. The *English Review* had some starry contributors: Conrad aside, others included Wells, James and Galsworthy and from the previous generation, Thomas Hardy. Ford's genius for networking need never be underestimated.

Inevitably Conrad and Ford fell out. Conrad had been writing his reminiscences for the magazine for seven months. Gout prevented him from supplying copy for July; Ford moved into melodramatic overdrive: 'We regret that owing to the serious illness of Mr Joseph Conrad we are compelled to postpone the publication of the next instalment of his Reminiscences.'

Although details are obscure, Conrad was clearly upset and refused to offer further instalments. Ford went on to the front foot, accusing Conrad of breaking faith. This elicited a rather grand response from Conrad which, unusually for him, veers perilously close to pomposity: 'You think I have discredited you and the Review, why then it must be even so. And as far as the Editor of the ER is concerned, we will let it go at that…'

The relationship with Ford never recovered. Conrad saw him as 'a megalomaniac who imagines that he is managing the universe'.

In the meantime, Conrad had put aside *Chance* and was working assiduously on his novel of Russian revolutionaries, *Razumov*, soon to be retitled *Under Western Eyes*.

As ever, he kept going, despite his frustration with the reading public, a frustration that could turn swiftly to animosity. In 1908, he notes with asperity: 'I have just received the accounts of all my publishers, from which I perceive that in all my immortal works (13 in all) have brought me last year something under five pounds in royalties.' Nor was he too aloof to avoid getting stuck into writers like Hall Caine and Marie Corelli who 'are very popular with the public' and 'also puffed in the press'. 'There are no lasting qualities in their work. The thought is commonplace and the style without any distinction. They are popular because they express the common thought, and the common man is delighted to find himself in accord with people he supposes distinguished.'

Conrad continued to borrow from Pinker, or Galsworthy, or indeed anyone else who was prepared to help. He needed money for Borys' school fees, rent for the house, furniture instalments, etc, etc. Debts mounted and he was even prepared to admit: 'perhaps I don't count strictly enough. When one does not see what one spends one is apt to spend too much.' Finally, with Pinker's help, and a £200 grant from the Royal Literary Fund supported by Galsworthy and Wells, Conrad pulled through.

1908 had begun badly with further attacks of gout and a worsening of Jessie's condition. Conrad kept wrestling with *Razumov*, which he summarised neatly to Galsworthy as follows:

> The Student Razumov (a natural son of a Prince K) gives up secretly to the police his fellow student, Haldin, who seeks refuge in his rooms after committing a political crime (supposed to be the murder of de Plehve.) First movement in St Petersburg (Haldin is hanged of course).
>
> 2nd [movement] in Genève. The Student Razumov meeting abroad the mother and sister of Haldin falls in love with that last, marries her, and, after a time, confesses to her the part he played in the arrest and death of her brother.
>
> The psychological developments leading to Razumov's betrayal of Haldin, to the confession of the fact to his wife and to the death of these people... form the real subject of the story.

Conrad was to modify the slightly sentimental second part as presented here, toughening Haldin's eventual fate. The novel grew over two years from a projected 62,000 words to an eventual 113,000; eventually it was finished in December 1909.

Under Western Eyes is regarded by some as an undisputed masterpiece. In many ways, it is an unusual novel. It resembles *Lord Jim* in that it examines the crime and (self) punishment of a central protagonist through the eyes of a sceptical observer, in this case, the teacher of languages. But whereas *Lord Jim* was influenced by both Maupassant and Flaubert, the presiding, (indeed brooding) presence who looms over *Under Western Eyes* is Dostoyevsky.

On the surface this is puzzling, because Conrad could not abide the Russian writer, largely because he was so intensely Russian: 'Moreover I don't know what Dostoyevsky stands for or reveals but I do know that he is too Russian for me. It sounds to me like some fierce mouthings from prehistoric ages.'

Although something of an oversimplification, there is a suspicion that in this novel Conrad is returning to semi-autobiographical material: he squares up again to betrayal, and to the Russians, who were the oppressors both of his people and of his parents. Unfortunately, even a novelist of Conrad's stature is hard pushed to take on Dostoyevsky and emerge unscathed.

Throughout the novel, Conrad denigrates all aspects of Russian life, despite retaining sympathy for his hero, Razumov. The relentless scorn which suited the fictional citizens of Costaguana, and the terrorists' denizens of London, sits less comfortably when applied to an entire nation. *Heart of Darkness* demonstrated how badly we, in the West, could behave. Yet Conrad appears to give his teacher of languages fulsome support when he stresses how primitive Russia is, and always has been, and how it contrasts so markedly with the West, with its civilised values and its concern for freedom:

> In its pride of numbers, in its strange pretensions of sanctity and in the secret readiness to abase itself in suffering, the spirit of Russia is the spirit of cynicism. It informs the declarations of statesmen, the theories of her revolutionists and the mystic vaticinations of prophets to the point of making freedom look like a form of debauch, and the Christian virtues themselves appear actually indecent.

Although this stuff has a fractious rhetorical energy, it is not really 'proven' by the story of Razumov's betrayal of Haldin. It remains an unsubstantiated generalisation that allows the reader to disagree.

Of course, there are moments of considerable power. Razumov (whose name is the genitive plural of the Russian *razum*, meaning intellect or reason) works hard at his studies to impress his father Prince K. As he is illegitimate, he can never impress his father sufficiently. This has autobiographical significance, clearly enough, and in *Victory* (1915) Conrad explores further the son who fails his father.

When Razumov finds himself isolated by his act of betrayal the prose begins to bite:

> Razumov longed desperately for a word of advice, for moral support. Who knows what true loneliness is – not the conventional word, but the naked terror? To the lonely themselves it wears a mask. The most miserable outcast hugs some memory or some illusion. Now and then a fatal conjunction of events may lift the veil for an instant. For an instant only. No human being could bear a steady view of moral solitude without going mad.

Unlike the anti-Slavic diatribes, Razumov's isolation is dramatised within the novel. It is hard to avoid speculating that Conrad himself felt estranged from his own life, despite the conventional comforts of family and friends.

Among his new friends was Agnes Tobin, a rich Californian poet and patron who introduced him to a group of young French writers, including André Gide, who constituted something of an elite fan club. Indeed, *Under Western Eyes* was dedicated to her and her 'genius for friendship'. André Gide remained on good terms with Conrad for many years, going so far as to buy John a Meccano set. John had fun with this, but his father found it frustrating, because his gouty hands could not cope with the fiddly bits.

After the completion of *Under Western Eyes*, Conrad rowed again with his agent and then suffered some kind of physical and depressive breakdown. Jessie wrote to his publisher:

The novel is finished but the penalty has to be paid. Months of nervous strain have ended in a complete nervous breakdown. Poor Conrad is very ill and Dr Hackney says it will be a long time before he is fit for anything requiring mental exertion... [The manuscript] lays on the table at the foot of his bed and he lives mixed up in the scenes and holds converse with the characters.

No further evidence is required of Conrad's self-destructive involvement in his creative work. When he recovered he wrote to Norman Douglas: 'I am all of a shake yet; I feel like a man returned from hell and look upon the very world of the living with dread.' In June 1910 the Conrads moved once more, this time to Capel House, an isolated farmhouse near Ashford, Kent.

In the following year or so Conrad continued to collect acquaintances. Richard Curle, a young columnist on the *Daily Mail*, was an adherent of Conrad's work and philosophy, described by his own son as a gloomy man subject to fits of melancholy and driven by irrational guilt. Conrad got on with him just fine. Curle returned the favour by fanning Conrad's reputation in the years of its decline, in the late twenties and thirties.

More bizarrely, Conrad was introduced to the fringes of the Bloomsbury group. Lady Ottoline Morrell was keen to meet him, to the horror of Henry James, who still regarded Conrad as a sophisticated artist trapped in the body of a rough foreign tar. Morrell's salon was a byword for liberal opinion and lax morals. Morrell herself had slept with Roger Fry, Augustus John and Bertrand Russell. Unsurprisingly, she had a keen eye for surfaces:

Conrad's appearance was really that of a Polish nobleman. His manner was perfect, almost too elaborate... He talked English with a strong accent, as if he tasted his words in his mouth before pronouncing them; but he talked extremely well, though he always had the talk and manner of a foreigner.

Conrad evinced little enthusiasm for Morrell and her merry crew of like-minded intellectual folk; he would be quick to realise that he was being patronised, in the worst sense. He did pick up one genuine admirer though. Bertrand Russell gushed to Morrell in terms that would not shame a teenage groupie, how much he loved Conrad. Why the co-author of *Principia Mathematica* should be so smitten, remains something of a puzzle: perhaps he recognised that Conrad shared something of his own frustration. In his *Autobiography* Russell noted that, in social situations, he felt like a fish in an aquarium: constantly banging his nose on the glass, ever aware of the invisible barrier that separated him from others.

Conrad was delighted to be courted by a member of the British aristocracy and was flattered when Russell named his son after him: 'Of all the incredible things that come to pass this – that there should be one day a Russell bearing mine for one of his names is surely the most marvellous.' For a moment, Conrad felt accepted.

Under Western Eyes was published on 5th October 1911, with a British print run of 3,000 copies. This is not a large number, but the reviewers suggested that there was, at long last, a shift in critical perspective.

Conrad's problem with the critics was that he became increasingly difficult to pigeonhole. He was known initially as a writer of exotic tales of faraway places, only to shift into the role of prose poet of the sea. Just as the reviewers were getting their heads around that, he then pitched in with *Heart of Darkness*, *Nostromo* and *The Secret Agent*. Lost, they then tended to fall back on stock clichés about fine writing and convoluted plot construction.

Above all, *Under Western Eyes* was praised both as a sophisticated commentary on the Russian novel – Constance Garnett's translations of Tolstoy and Dostoyevsky were emerging at this time, so Russian novels were fashionable – and for its psychological penetration. The *Morning Post* described it as a 'convincing study of soul in the cruel, remorseless grip of fate', whilst the *Pall Mall Gazette* regarded it as 'remarkable' for its psychological insight; though the *Gazette*, possibly in a mild fit of xenophobia, drew attention to the Polish author's grammatical errors.

Later Conrad
1911–21

In the meantime Conrad was at work on *Chance*, his next novel; he had just published some more reminiscences (under the oblique title *A Personal Record*) and was keen to keep his name before the public. At home, despite the usual minor ailments, there was relative peace. Borys, who was now thirteen, needed further education and Conrad decided that he should attend HMS *Worcester*, a nautical school ship. Like many parents leaving their children at boarding school, Conrad's feelings were mixed:

> B looked to me a very small and lonely figure on that enormous deck in that big crowd where he didn't know a single soul. It is an immense change for him. Yes. He did look a small boy. I couldn't make up my mind to leave him and at last I made rather a bolt of it. I can't get him out of my eyes...

Whatever Conrad's shortcomings as a father, his affection for both his sons is never in doubt.

On 12th December 1911 he was nearing the end of *Chance* and wrote to Pinker:

> I see my end right enough but the putting it down with some effect is the very devil. And of course I have ominous twinges of toothache. Ever since *Lord Jim* (inclusive) the

end of every long novel has cost me a tooth. I wouldn't mind losing two teeth to get this done quickly.

This is writing experienced as a form of physical torture.

One of the assumptions of professional Conrad criticism is that, with *Chance*, his work spirals into a sharp decline. There are some votes for the later *Victory*, a few more for the novella *The Shadow-Line*, but there is general agreement that his decision to focus on 'love' stories in his later years was a catastrophic misjudgement. The explanation for this supposed artistic suicide is that, after years of ferocious concentration, he was weary, burnt out, past it.

This theory of artistic mismanagement, and of its root cause, is both naive and simplistic. Once again, Conrad is being berated for failing to repeat himself.

In his later work, from the excellent story 'A Smile of Fortune' onward, Conrad is writing 'romances'. He is consciously using Shakespeare as his model: and there are elements of both *Chance* and *Victory* which consciously mirror *The Winter's Tale* and, especially, *The Tempest*. It does not need a genius to understand that the later novels lack the self-lacerating personal and political analysis of *Nostromo* and *The Secret Agent*; but there is a wry gentleness and a touching belief in the possibility of redemption that is neither strained, nor superficial.

'A Smile of Fortune' sets the pattern with a young girl and her manipulative father, who both set out to capture a young captain who while narrating the story, shrouds his own actions in an impenetrable halo of moral ambiguity. There are shades here of Prospero, Miranda and Ferdinand.

In *Chance*, through an elaborate superstructure of narrators we are again confronted with an errant father, an innocent/ignorant young girl and a dithering suitor.

One of these narrators is Marlow, who returns for his final curtain call. As before, his role is complex. During much of the novel he spews out the same misogynist nonsense previously heard in *Heart of Darkness*; but much as he may insist that women 'are devoid of decency' the actions of Flora de Barral prove otherwise. His flailing generalisations demonstrate in crisp fashion that to live life you have eventually to commit yourself to other people: sniping on the sidelines may give one an illusion of superiority, but it is an illusion only.

The heroine's problem is that her father, a convicted swindler of spectacular proportions, puts her outside the pale of society. When she meets an adoring admirer, in the shape of Captain Anthony, she cannot really understand what he is feeling; and he, in turn, is so diffident that he cannot find either the words or gestures to express himself. This mutual incomprehension makes painful reading. The characters are victims of the determining powers of nature and nurture: the title *Chance* is purely ironic.

The novel proved to be an astonishing success, and freed Conrad from the financial servitude that had crippled his life. The reasons for the book's triumph are simple, but Conrad's friends and contemporaries tended to affect puzzlement. Garnett suggested in curmudgeonly fashion that 'the figure of the lady on the "jacket" did more to bring the novel into favour than a long review by Sir Sidney Colvin in *The Observer*'.

In fact, the proprietor of the *New York Herald* decided to serialise the book and this, in turn, persuaded Alfred Knopf, who worked for Doubleday, to put the full weight of promotional advertising behind Conrad's book, making it a fashionable 'read'. That apart, the novel had at its core a love story that was both melodramatic yet intelligently tender – surely enough to ensure popularity.

The only blot on this particularly sunny horizon was the review by Henry James. Even at this stage of his career, Conrad regarded James with considerable awe: indeed, he was probably the only living author whom Conrad could admire unreservedly.

In typical fashion, James tiptoes around his objections to the book before spelling them out, in a manner so archly convoluted as to border on the parodic. The central thrust is that he dislikes the use of different narrators, which he believes obfuscates the story without enlightening the reader. They form:

> successive members of a cue from one to the other of which the sense and the interest of the subject have to be passed on together, in the manner of the buckets of water for the improvised extinction of a fire, before reaching our apprehension: all with whatever result, to this apprehension, of a quantity to be allowed for as spilt by the way.

Conrad later confided that of all the mediocre reviews he had been awarded down the years – and they were legion – this was the only one to have 'affected him painfully'.

Whatever the force of the rebuff, Conrad's new financial status was signalled by the purchase of a second hand Cadillac. According to Borys, who loved cars all his life, his mother was a competent driver, calmly taking difficulties in her stride; this was in marked contrast to his father who tended to over-react, jamming the brakes on hard at the slightest opportunity.

Conrad moaned to Gide: 'I well know I have written myself out.' But he continued to work on various short stories, even sending Pinker a sketchy outline of *Victory*, his last important novel: 'an unconventional man and a girl on an island under peculiar circumstance to whom enters a gang of three ruffians also of a rather unconventional sort – this intrusion producing certain psychological developments and effects – there is philosophy in it and also drama – lightly treated – meant for cultured people.'

This bald outline could be a plot summary for *The Tempest*: and the final aesthetic and moral purpose 'meant for cultured people' would similarly seem to link the novel with Shakespeare's last play.

Meanwhile Conrad was on a roll. As *Chance* was being serialised, a collection of short stories *Twixt Land and Sea* was unanimously praised and the English edition of 3,500 copies ensured that it was Conrad's largest print run to date.

Despite his notorious diffidence, and sudden switches of mood, Conrad enjoyed socialising, albeit at his own pace. He came to know Arnold Bennett, a writer whose estimation of Maupassant was as high as his own; and Bennett was one of the few to recognise the importance of *Nostromo*. He also introduced Conrad to Joseph Retinger. Retinger, son of a Cracow lawyer, educated in Paris, had come to London on a political mission to gather support for the cause of Polish independence. He probably hoped to enlist Conrad's help, but the old sceptic was never likely to be found waving a banner for any political cause, no matter how worthy. Retinger's wife, Otolia, was young and attractive.

Early in 1913 she and her husband stayed at Capel House:

[Conrad] was also fond of talking about literature; his favourite authors were the French masters of the word whom he admired. On those occasions he liked to speak French. In English he always had a marked foreign accent. He spoke Polish clearly with a charming Ukrainian accent. Sometimes, unable to find some word, he would switch into French.

Recently, Conrad has been accused of plagiarism on a minor scale, as scholars have eagerly scanned his works for phrases and paragraphs pinched from Gallic authors, major and minor. As noted, the debt to Maupassant in *The Nigger of the Narcissus* is strong: but apart from that, the evidence points towards Conrad picking up phrases and assimilating them as his own as he moved, almost unconsciously, between one language and anther. Otolia Retinger's testimony certainly throws a dubious light on his assertion that he always thought in English once he had joined the Merchant Service. When in relaxed company, and not playing his role of Kentish squire, he could be fluently polyglot.

The Retingers helped Conrad think again about his relationship with his native country. This was to have near fatal consequences in the following year.

Throughout 1913, Conrad was at work on *Victory* and, as usual, he hopelessly underestimated its length and complexity. His efforts only slowed for the usual bouts of family illness. On 1st July the novel was given its title, but then Conrad went back and fussed over the first three parts of the book. When completed, he managed to negotiate some fat contracts and he was paid the stratospheric sum of £1,850 for the serialisation and advances for the book edition. For the first time since leaving Poland, he was earning the sort of money that he felt was his due. With his head now high, and with the encouragement of the Retingers, he decided it was time to take a family break and return to his native land. Even in terms of Conrad's usual catastrophic holidays, this one was to prove rather special. The Conrads – all four – and the Retingers finally set forth on 25th July 1914, three days before war broke out between Austria and Serbia, and a week or so before the outbreak of the Great War itself.

On the surface, it seems strange that an acute political observer like Conrad could have missed the signs of trouble that were piling up throughout the spring of 1914. But Conrad had little or no interest in the daily ups and downs of politicians; he approached politics as socio-anthropological phenomenon. Even so, it was a colossal blunder.

Conrad was to write an account of his Polish visit, but as so often in his attempts at autobiography, he sanitised events to suit his view of himself as a returned exile.

As war buzzed around them, movement was difficult, but not impossible. Conrad enjoyed meeting people and was sunnily self absorbed. He wrote to Pinker on 8th August:

My health is good. I am getting a mental stimulus out of this affair – I can tell you! And if it were not for the unavoidable anxiety I would derive much benefit from the experience.

At this stage Britain and Germany had been at war for four days.

Although not widely known in Poland, Conrad was courted as something of an exotic. Obviously enough, he now participated actively in discussion about Poland's future, but one or two of his hosts found his 'phlegmatic composure' a little irritating. They wanted him to declare himself a patriot, obviously enough. But he would remain cautious about the possibility of Poland's independence.

Jessie found the Polish experience beyond her. On arriving in Cracow she found 'the road paving extremely primitive and the odour of stables and bad draining was something sickening. Conrad noticed my expression. He turned to me rather sharply, remarking: "This is not England, my dear don't expect too much."' Jessie was later to write that much of her husband's behaviour, which seemed to her initially unfathomable, was explicable in terms of Polish national characteristics.

Conrad took Borys to the Jagiellonian Library in Cracow. Here they were shown Conrad's father's manuscripts and letters, all of which Conrad had believed lost. They visited Apollo's grave which bore the stern reminder 'Victim of Muscovite Tyranny'. Here, for possibly the only time in Conrad's adulthood, he knelt in prayer.

As a nationalised British citizen, Conrad risked internment by the Austrian authorities. He was also running out of money and his gout made an unwelcome reappearance. Conrad decided to leave for Vienna. After a hair-raising journey across country, which scared the wits out of Jessie, they arrived on 10th October 1914, in a train packed with wounded soldiers. Even though he was now crippled with pain, Conrad was keen to discuss the Polish question with any available eminence grise who would listen.

From Vienna, the family travelled to Milan, from Milan to Genoa – where a spot of sightseeing was in order – and from Genoa they arrived home. Meanwhile the Great War rumbled on.

They reached London on 2nd November. Conrad was bubbling with schemes to involve Britain in the matter of Poland. Two days later Arnold Bennett noted in his diary, with some asperity, that Conrad wanted England to influence public opinion favourably towards Austria. 'As if he could.'

Victory was published in instalments during February 1915, in book form in the United States the following month. The novel is often underestimated: Conrad returns to his old settings, and old themes, but he treats them in entirely new ways.

The central figure of the novel, Axel Heyst, has isolated himself on a Malayan island, a victim of his father's sceptical philosophy and morose influence: 'he had perceived the means of passing through life without suffering and almost without a single care in the world – invulnerable because elusive.'

Unfortunately Heyst becomes entangled with life – it has him 'fairly by the throat' – as he becomes involved first in a speculative business venture, then with Lena, whom he rescues from an itinerant band that tours the archipelago 'entertaining' sailors.

Once Heyst whisks her off to his magical island, he has nothing to say to her. The great love scenes beneath the Eastern moon cannot take place because Heyst's emotional sterility cuts too deep. When Lena is upset, Heyst's response is helpless bafflement: 'I don't even understand what I have done or left undone to distress you like this.'

Eventually, three villains invade the island, to return Lena to Schomberg, the bar-owner who is keen to become Lena's lover. In the ensuring debacle, Lena is killed, protecting Heyst. The suggestion is that, unable to give Heyst love, she gives him death instead. The nature of her victory is thrown further into question when Heyst commits suicide, unable to live with her sacrifice.

In the novel, Conrad treats sexual relations with a subtlety that recalls Henry James at his finest. But the stifling sense of repression, the grim reflections on loneliness, are Conrad's own. Despite the bleak conclusion, the potential value of romantic love is never questioned. Along with *Chance*, it must therefore rank as one of the most optimistic of his major works.

Possibly the reading public sensed this: the novel sold an unbelievable 11,000 copies in the first three days. The reviews were all positive: *The New York Times*, spotting the Shakespearian undercurrent that flows through much of the late work, felt that Heyst was a sort of Malay Hamlet; Walter de la Mare, writing for the *Times Literary Supplement*, described the novel (rather affectedly) as 'a little dish of diamonds'.

It was difficult for Conrad to savour his triumph. On his second attempt, Borys had passed the entrance exam for Sheffield University. Unfortunately, he decided to volunteer for the Army. With the help of Conrad's old friend Cunninghame Graham, Borys was granted a commission. He was seventeen and a half: on 20th September he was re-enrolled as a second lieutenant. Eventually he was sent to the Western Front where he was gassed: he also suffered shell shock, and was hospitalised.

In the early months of his son's service, it was hard for Conrad to grasp what was really going on. Like many sons writing to their parents, Borys could maintain an attitude of merry insouciance. As Conrad wrote to Galsworthy with evident pride:

> Borys is in command of the advanced detachment and sees his Captain only once or twice a week… He writes cheerfully boyish letters in the same tone as his Worcester correspondence. We send him a tuck-box now and again. It's as if he were still at school.

Throughout the war, Conrad had a grim time, like everyone else and, like everyone else, he was a zealous patriot. A strong indication of this was his reaction to the trial of his former Congo companion Roger Casement.

Casement had become an Irish Nationalist. He tried to gather support for 'the cause' in America and subsequently travelled to

Germany in November 1914. At the time of the Easter Rebellion in 1916, the Germans landed him on the Irish coast. He was captured, tried and convicted of treason in June 1916. He appealed against the death sentence but the appeal was rejected, and in August he was executed.

Conrad was implacably unsympathetic. In a letter to an Irish Nationalist who was attempting to gather support for Casement between his arrest and trial, Conrad rewrites the past without a flicker of remorse:

> We never talked politics. I didn't think he had really any...
> He was a good companion; but already in Africa I judged
> that he was a man, properly speaking, of no mind at all.
> I don't mean stupid. I mean that he was all emotion. By
> emotional force he made his way, and sheer temperament –
> a truly tragic personality: all but the greatness of which he
> had not a trace. Only vanity. But in the Congo it was not
> visible yet.

Conrad refused to sign a circulated appeal for pardon and expressed more than once his vehement dislike for an individual whom he came to regard as a dangerous (because stupid) idealist.

1916 brought some interest in the comely shape of Jane Anderson, an American journalist born in Atlanta, who had a penchant for powerful middle-aged men. She soon became chummy with H.G. Wells and as a fan of Conrad's work, she hoped that Wells might inveigle an invitation for her to visit Capel House. After a bit more effort she finally succeeded, and wrote an enthusiastic account of her first meeting. She clearly found Conrad attractive:

> It is the pose of his head that gives the impression of
> strength. His mouth, although not clearly defined under the
> grey moustache is full but sensitive. But it is the eyes which
> are the eyes of genius. They are dark, and the lids droop

except in moments of intense excitement. They are dark brown… and there is in them a curious hypnotic quality.

Anderson pinged with sexual vivacity. Conrad was obviously flattered by the attention, and Jessie, initially, liked her. When writing of her, Conrad tended to move into a linguistic register that is, frankly, un-Conradian:

> We made the acquaintance of a new young woman. She comes from Arizona and (strange to say!) she has a European mind. She is seeking to get herself adopted as our own big daughter and is succeeding fairly. To put it shortly, she's quite yum-yum.

She visited regularly and John enjoyed her company as much as his father, once commenting on her legs. As time wore on it is not hard to suspect that Jessie grew peeved. Jessie was overweight and mildly disabled: Jane Anderson played her role of flame-haired temptress to the hilt, and beyond. Although the details are obscure, it is clear that Jessie challenged Conrad with a letter that he had sent to Jane, and that Conrad was embarrassed at being caught out. Without a word he tossed it onto the fire.

It is unlikely that Conrad had an affair with Anderson: she was twenty-eight, he was fifty-eight; she was highly sexed, Conrad aggressively diffident and crippled with gout. There was undoubtedly some heavy-duty flirtation, but given Conrad's natural reticence, it is unlikely that Conrad was unfaithful to Jessie. Biographers who are keen to posit this affair, underestimate the value Conrad placed upon fidelity whether to women, ships or art. In any case, Anderson eventually went on to have a liaison with Conrad's Polish friend Retinger, and helped to break up his marriage.

The only serious creative work Conrad undertook during the war years was the novella *The Shadow-Line*, which he dedicated to

Borys 'with love'. Just as in *Victory* he returned to the novels of the early Malay period, so in *The Shadow-Line*, he revisits the manner of 'Youth' and *The Nigger of the Narcissus*. The story is presented as semi-autobiographical and is subtitled 'A Confession'. It is Conrad's final masterpiece and the fitting conclusion to a life of toil, at sea, and behind the writing desk.

The opening paragraph glows with a nostalgia that is spiced by informality. Conrad, who has so often orchestrated his prose in the most lurid colours available to him, now speaks to the reader with unaffected casualness:

> Only the young have such moments. I don't mean the very young. No. The very young have, properly speaking, no moments. It is the privilege of early youth to live in advance of its days in all the beautiful continuity of hope which knows no pauses and no introspection.

The achieved simplicity suggests that Conrad, facing his demons for the last time, has emerged battered, but mildly triumphant. No need now for multiple narrators; 'I' speaks to us directly, and we are to assume his name to be 'Conrad'.

In the 'Author's Note', Conrad indirectly links the trial of his 'younger' self, as he passes the shadow-line from youth to maturity, with the suffering that Borys' generation were to endure in the trenches, and elsewhere:

> Nobody can doubt that before the supreme trial of a whole generation I had an acute consciousness of the minute and insignificant character of my own obscure experience. There could be no question here of any parallelism. That notion never entered my head. But there was a feeling of identity...

The story fictionalises Conrad's first command. Although simple virtues of courage and fidelity are upheld, the new captain also has to deal with a crisis which, though not his fault, elicits from him extreme, and often baffling, guilt. Conrad's recognition that guilt can be rootless, and that it must be borne all the same, gives this story an edge lacking in simpler stories like 'Typhoon' and 'Youth'. In the end the command proves a success, as the narrator comes to terms with his own psychological and moral imperfections whilst in the process growing up:

'But I'll tell you, Captain Giles, how I feel. I feel old. And I must be. All of you on shore look to me just a lot of skittish youngsters that have never known a care in the world.'

He didn't smile. He looked insufferably exemplary. He declared:

'That will pass. But you do look older – it's a fact.'

'Aha!' I said.

'No! No! The truth is that one must not make too much of anything in life, good or bad.'

'Live at half-speed,' I murmured perversely. 'Not everybody can do that.'

Conrad wanted to take some part in the war and, with the help of the Admiralty, he visited British ports to witness naval activities. Whether this was to boost the morale of the seamen, or of Conrad, is unclear. He even flew from the Air Station in Yarmouth which, given his age, his state of health, and the precariousness of early aircraft, shows considerable gumption. He avoided telling Jessie about this particular episode.

He worked away on this and that, and dictated at speed *The Arrow of Gold*, which was something of a pot-boiler. Although Conrad could never re-read it without a tear and trembling lip, it offers few joys for the modern reader. Indeed, it is clichéd from start to finish and must be one of the worst books ever by a major writer. By its side, Lawrence's *The Plumed Serpent* seems a disciplined masterwork.

The novel recalls Conrad's Marseille adventures and details M. George's love for the mysterious Rita de Lastoala. Her mysteriousness is ladled out so relentlessly that she seldom aspires to two dimensions; Conrad's prose reads like the work of a lazy parodist:

> The white stairs, the deep crimson of the carpet, and the light blue of the dress made an effective combination of colour to set off the delicate carnation of the face, which, after the first glance given to the whole person, drew irresistibly your gaze to itself by an indefinable quality of charm beyond all analysis and made you think of remote races, of strange generations, of the faces of women sculptured on immemorial monuments and of those lying unsung in their tombs.

It is scarcely credible that Conrad had completed *The Shadow-Line* only a few months before.

Although Conrad was relieved with the signing of the Armistice – for one thing Borys had survived – on Armistice Day itself, he was on full apocalyptic throttle: 'I cannot confess to an easy mind. Great and blind forces are set free catastrophically all over the world…'

The brightest political glimmer on the horizon was the granting of Poland's independence, though Conrad grumbled vociferously that the Bolsheviks were to be granted a voice at the Peace Conference.

Jessie continued to have treatment for her knee, as the family moved from Capel House to Spring Grove near Wye and finally to Oswald's, just outside Canterbury. They remained here until Conrad's death.

During 1919 Conrad did not really settle to work, though he finally managed to complete *The Rescue*, a reheated Malayan story that had been simmering away since the 1890s. All the usual exotic apparatus is apparent: crafty Malays, noble Rajahs, a glamorous princess and the sea robber Daman, with his 'vengeful heart and the eyes of a gazelle'.

Although Conrad was always eager to impart to friends the poor state of his health, from the beginning of the 1920s he complains of feeling worn out. Writing to Galsworthy, he admits: 'I am less crippled now but I feel shaky and mentally tired – and truly there is little reason for the last…'

He began working on his Napoleonic novel *Suspense*, but the research seemed to take on a life of its own, dousing his creativity.

As ever when he felt low, he suggested to Jessie that they take a holiday. You would think they would have learned their lesson. This time they left for Corsica, leaving in the new year of 1921, 'in search of climate'. They were joined by the Pinkers, staying at the Grand Hotel in Ajaccio.

Of course, the weather was foul. 'Cold. Wet. Horrors.' Conrad was bad tempered and miserable and, despite being joined by his secretary, little was accomplished on the big Napoleonic book. He even found that the mountains got on his nerves. At the beginning of April the Conrads returned home.

Towards Death
1921–4

For the remainder of 1921 Conrad laboured away at *Suspense*. On 21st December, he informed Pinker that he had managed 5,500 words on a new effort, a short story which would also have a Napoleonic background. This evolved into *The Rover*, his last novel.

In some respects, this boy's book for grownups constitutes a self-conscious farewell. It tells of the retired sailor Peyrol who for the sake of honour and patriotism is prepared to undertake one final adventure. Conrad's prose is once again tight and the Provençal landscapes are sharply delineated:

> There were leaning pines on the skyline, and in the pass itself silvery green patches of olive orchards below a long yellow wall backed by dark cypresses, and the red roofs of buildings which seemed to belong to a farm.

This is quite unlike the descriptions of the Malay novels, or indeed *Heart of Darkness*. Conrad is not aiming for metaphysical significance, but for immediate visual impact. It should come as no surprise that Hemingway was a fond admirer: he clearly learned a great deal from the later, leaner Conrad.

Whilst at work on the book, Conrad learned of Pinker's death of pneumonia at the age of fifty-eight. As Conrad's agent, Pinker had endured much. Conrad wrote to his son: 'Twenty years' friendship and for most of that time in the constant interchange of the most intimate thoughts and feelings created a bond as strong as the nearest relationship.'

In the spring of 1923, Conrad embarked on his last long journey. At the invitation of Frank Doubleday, his publisher, Conrad agreed to visit the United States, to meet his adoring public. On 21st April he set sail on the 26,000 ton *Tuscania*. Conrad found life aboard the cruise-ship disagreeable. He disliked the 'attempts at all kinds of sham comforts, all the disadvantages of a gregarious life, with the added worry of not being able to get away from it'.

Nor did he much enjoy his arrival. Writing home, he fulminates:

> I will not attempt to describe to you my landing, because it is indescribable. To be aimed at by forty cameras held by forty men that look as if they came in droves is a nerve shattering experience…

Conrad refused to lecture formally, possibly because he was self-conscious about his accent, possibly because he thought that he would not be sufficiently entertaining; but he did agree to give a talk and a reading, and intoned the final pages of *Victory*. His account to Jessie gives final proof, if any were needed, that she remained the love of his life, despite the disbelief of his friends and the incredulity of future biographers:

> After the applause from the audience, which stood up when I appeared, had ceased I had a moment of positive anguish. Then I took out the watch you had given me and laid it on the table and made one mighty effort and began to speak. That watch was the greatest comfort to me. Something of you?

Conrad was lionised by the rich and the influential. By the time he returned to England, he was exhausted.

And exceedingly annoyed. On his return he discovered that Borys had secretly married a young woman that he had met in France, in an officers' canteen. Jessie decided to avoid troubling Conrad with this revelation until he had finished his tour of the States. Predictably, he was enraged if Jessie's account is to be trusted:

> He interrupted me with scant ceremony. 'I don't want to know anything more about it. It is done and I have been treated like a blamed fool...'

In May 1924, the socialist Prime Minister offered a knighthood. Possibly following the lead of Galsworthy and Kipling, perhaps believing himself to be sufficiently aristocratic already, Conrad turned it down.

Not that he was averse to honours, especially if they entailed a financial reward. He pinned great hopes on winning the Nobel, especially with the publication of *The Rover*. It never happened. He joined the list of Nobel failures that includes Hardy, Joyce, Woolf, Lawrence, Twain, James, Proust and Tolstoy.

Conrad was now battling chronic ill health. Ford tried a rapprochement and hoped that Conrad might contribute to his new magazine. Conrad did not feel up to it, and was tired of Ford whom he came to regard as both selfish and demanding. He had sufficient bile in him to describe him as a 'swelled-headed creature who seems to imagine that he will sweep all Europe and devastate Great Britain with an eventual collected edition of his works'.

The saddest account of Conrad's final months comes from Jacob Epstein, who was commissioned to sculpt him. The bust is a powerful representation of a man who has looked at life squarely and felt unimpressed. Epstein found Conrad crippled, depressed and 'played out'. He was toying with an unfinished manuscript – which was *Suspense*, his uncompleted last novel.

His health continued to decline. There was a mild heart attack, further bouts of feverish illness, the inevitable onset of gout. He told Curle that he would not be sorry to die. He wrote to a friend: 'I haven't been well for a long time and strictly entre nous I begin to feel like a cornered rat.'

On 1st August, Conrad took Curle out to see a new house he was hoping to rent (on the move once again) when he suffered a heart attack. Initially diagnosed as indigestion, it became clear, the following day, that he was very ill indeed. On the evening of the 2nd, he whispered to Borys that he knew that he really was unwell 'this time'. At 8.30 the following morning, a Sunday, he called to Jessie who was in the adjoining room, recovering from one of her many operations. His wife heard him cry out: 'Here' or 'here you.' There was a crash. Conrad's heart had given out and he had fallen to the floor. He died suddenly on 3rd August 1924, aged sixty-six.

Apart from the brief moment at his father's graveside when he prayed in deference to his father's beliefs, Conrad showed no interest in Christianity or its forms of worship: 'It's strange how I always, from the age of fourteen, disliked the Christian religion, its doctrines, ceremonies and festivals.'

Nevertheless, like many quiescent atheists, he was given a Christian, specifically Catholic, burial, organised by Jessie, who was unable to attend because of her disability. It took place during the Canterbury cricket festival: the mourners having to look suitably solemn amidst a riot of flags and bunting. Among those present was Edward Raczynski, the only official, and a representative of the Polish government. One French fan angry at the prevailing philistinism of the British remarked tartly: 'had Anatole France, died, all Paris would have been at his funeral.' No doubt the Dean of Canterbury made up for it, describing Conrad as a 'great and noble-minded man'.

On Conrad's tombstone his name was muddled into neither Polish or English. It is Joseph Teodor Korzeniowski: an emblem of the confusions that shadowed his life. Also engraved is the epigraph he used for *The Rover*:

Sleep after Toyle, port after stormie seas,
Ease after warre, death after life, does greatly please.

The lines are from Spenser's *Faerie Queene*: Great Despaire is counselling suicide.

Jessie lived on, in various stages of infirmity, arguing with Borys, looking after Conrad's estate and enjoying tea at the Curzon. Although remarkably resilient she described herself, at sixty, as a 'lonely woman'. She died at sixty-three, in 1936, and was buried next to her husband.

Reviewing Conrad's life, it is as difficult to get to grips with his moody, neurotic personality as it is with his courageous intelligence. He was unsparing on himself and pretty tough on others. In his letters he came across as a mixture of tortured artist and perpetual whiner, but he was capable of piercing humour: almost all of his novels have moments of ferocious banter, where the ironic vision is thrown so acutely over a situation, that the reader is reduced to mirthless laughter.

Without doubt Conrad was, even in youth, awkward and irascible. Fearing his own inner chaos, he chose the life of the sailor to give him the discipline he needed; when boredom set in, he chose the rigours of the novelist's art, applying himself with a monk-like devotion to the creation of fiction unlike anything seen before in Anglo-American literature. His dedication to his task makes even Henry James seem something of a slacker; the intensity of his work might make even Joyce boggle.

Conrad wrenched the English novel out of its bourgeois preoccupation with love, marriage and finance. Like Kipling, he focused on the individual's relationship with work and duty. Unlike Kipling, he was fascinated with both betrayal and self-betrayal. In *Heart of Darkness* and *Nostromo*, he demonstrated clearly enough that ideals and beliefs can save neither an individual nor a society. The ruling passions of mankind are selfishness and self-delusion, topped up with a morbid dislike of the truth.

As a result, even the most decent of us are beset by isolation and loneliness. Society is a construct which offers us the consolation of false security: only when put to the test are we likely to be found wanting and whether that test occurs in the jungle of Africa or the streets of London is entirely immaterial.

Conrad spells this out to Cunninghame Graham:

The mysteries of a universe made of drops of fire and clods of blood do not concern us in the least. The fate of a humanity condemned ultimately to perish from cold is not worth troubling about. If you take it to heart it becomes an unendurable tragedy. If you believe in improvement you must weep, for the attained perfection must end in cold, darkness and silence. In a dispassionate view the ardour for reform, improvement, for virtue, for knowledge, and even beauty is only a vain sticking up for appearances as though one were anxious about the cut of one's clothes in a community of blind men.

Afterlife

Conrad's literary influence was pervasive. Although the readership of his novels declined after his death, he remained the writer's writer par excellence.

The arch-modernist T.S. Eliot set the pattern of appreciation, quoting Kurtz's last words as an epigraph to 'The Hollow Men'. The Americans, in any case, always revered Conrad. He struck them as an international, rather than a British writer. Scott Fitzgerald's Gatsby is a genial cousin to Kurtz, and the novel's narrator, Nick, is a more complacent Marlow: Gatsby's parties are a twenties re-imagining of *Heart of Darkness'* 'unspeakable rites'. Hemingway reinterpreted Conrad's emphasis on the solidarity of seamanship into something deliberately both more macho and more unreliable. Faulkner's use of multiple viewpoints and shifting time schemes owe much to *Nostromo* and *The Secret Agent*.

Writers as different as André Gide and Thomas Mann both admired Conrad and learned from him. Mann warmed to his 'cool objectivity', whilst Gide helped to translate and to supervise translations of various works into French. He was particularly interested in *Lord Jim*. Jim's jump, arguably, is the first existential act inspiring not only Gide, but his later co-workers in this field, Sartre and Camus.

In Britain, the influence of Conrad's writing is strong and thriving. Graham Greene's seedy landscapes and cityscapes begin in Mr Verloc's dubious shop. In *A Burnt Out Case* Greene pays direct homage to Conrad, opening with a steamer puffing up the Congo river. Malcolm Lowry's masterpiece *Under the Volcano* has the same applied linguistic density as *Nostromo*, similarly evoking exotic landscapes to underpin human corruption. Even Virginia Woolf seems to recognise Conrad's influence in the high rhetorical flourishes of the 'Time Passes' section of *To the Lighthouse* – which resembles passages of 'Youth', with fussy detail for added emphasis.

Of more recent writers, John Le Carré and William Golding obviously owe a debt to him. Le Carré's interest in betrayal and self-delusion tops even Graham Greene's, and his belief in the nature of 'the test' links his characters to Jim, Razumov and Heyst. Golding's exploration of solidarity, isolation and evil in *Rites of Passage* has a clear forerunner in *The Nigger of the Narcissus*: the James Wait and the Reverend Colley dying unmourned in their cabins, share a mysterious kinship.

Post-colonial writing is inspired and irritated by Conrad, in equal measure. *Heart of Darkness* remains a text that is contentious. For Chinua Achebe it represents all that is bogus about the European attitude towards Africa; for V.S. Naipaul, it proved the starting point for one of his finest novels, *A Bend in the River*. The Kenyan writer Ngugi wa Thiongo's novel *A Grain of Wheat* transposes the situation of *Under Western Eyes* to the recent history of the Kenyan struggle for independence. The loner Mungo, thought to be a hero, betrays Kihika to the British in order to save himself.

Conrad's strength as a novelist is that he cannot be placed in an Anglo-American tradition of novel writing, despite the efforts of F.R. Leavis in the 1940s. His scepticism, his corrosive irony, his dedication to exposing the flaws in people and the systems they build to protect themselves, are unique. He wrote of himself:

I have been called a writer of the sea, of the tropics, a descriptive writer, a romantic writer – and also a realist. But

as a matter of fact all my concern has been with the 'ideal'
value of things, events and people. That and nothing else.

Conrad's vindication has been the subsequent history of the
twentieth century and the opening years of the twenty-first.
Heart of Darkness continues to illuminate the regimes of terror
and barbarism which have afflicted the last hundred years;
Nostromo's warnings about the remorseless power of 'material
interests' are yet to be heeded in the Middle East; and the
inability of 'civilised' countries to understand or combat violent
terrorism effectively is the most devastating revelation of *The
Secret Agent*.

No other writer in recent times combines such acuity and
authority. As he had hoped in the preface to *The Nigger of the
Narcissus*, his finest legacy was:

> To arrest, for the space of a breath, the hands busy about
> the work of the earth, and compel men entranced by the
> sight of distant goals to glance for a moment at the
> surrounding vision of form and colour, of sunshine and
> shadows...

As he had hoped, Conrad makes us 'see'. Unfortunately, what we
'see' brings rarely either consolation or comfort: he gives us
a glimpse of what we would sooner forget, and what we forget
at our own peril.

Chronological list of works

Bibliography

Baines, Jocelyn, *Joseph Conrad: A Critical Biography* (London, 1960).

Conrad, Borys, *My Father: Joseph Conrad* (London, 1970).

Conrad, Jessie, *Joseph Conrad as I Knew Him* (London, 1926).

—, *Joseph Conrad and His Circle* (London, 1935).

Conrad, John, *Joseph Conrad: Times Remembered* (Cambridge, 1981).

Ford, Ford Madox, *Joseph Conrad: A Personal Remembrance* (London, 1924).

Hewitt, Douglas, *Conrad: A Reassessment* (Cambridge, 1952).

Jean-Aubry, Georges, *Joseph Conrad: Life and Letters* (London, 1927).

Leavis, F.R., *The Great Tradition: George Eliot, Henry James, Joseph Conrad* (London, 1948).

Najder, Zdzislaw, *Joseph Conrad: A Life* (Rochester, NY, 2007).